RENEW YOUR MIND FOR SUCCESS

TRANSFORM YOUR THINKING AND BUILD LASTING WEALTH

TANNIZIA GASPER

Copyright © 2023 by Tannizia Gasper

Published by Tannizia Gasper in Partnership with
Bold Publishing (https://denisenicholson.com/bold-publishing)

Book Design by Opeyemi Ikuborije

Manufactured in the United States of America

ISBN: 979-8-9883985-5-4

Library of Congress Control Number: 2023919255

Follow Tannizia Gasper

Social Media Outlets:

Facebook: tannizia@facebook.com
Instagram: tannizia@ig.com
Email: tannizia@tanniziagasper.com

Dedication

I want to express deep gratitude to my cheerleader, confidant, and champion, Mrs. Terrine Anthony, who inspired me to write this book. Her belief in my wildest dreams has guided me, and I repeatedly carried her unshakeable faith until I could prove it. Her attitude toward my goals is always, "Go for it." These words have become my guiding star and my purpose to endure through life's obstacles. Thank you, Mrs. Terrine Anthony.

My self-confidence comes from my mother's unfailing support. She taught me to recover from setbacks, heal my scars, and see life's challenges as opportunities for progress. My mother has taught me the strength of unwavering faith through her support. Her kindness has lifted me through life's storms and inspired me to follow my aspirations. This book is dedicated to my amazing mother, who has always loved and supported me. You've inspired me and shaped my path. Thank you for being my North Star.

Acknowledgement

I would like to express my deepest gratitude and appreciation to everyone who has helped to create "Renew Your Mind for Success." Without your assistance, encouragement, and insightful suggestions, this endeavor would not have been feasible. I want to begin by expressing my sincerest gratitude to my family, whose unwavering love and confidence in me have been a constant source of motivation. Your encouragement, patience, and understanding have been invaluable throughout the writing process. I am extremely appreciative of your unwavering support.

My mentors and advisors have guided me along this path of personal and professional development. Your wisdom, guidance, and expertise have shaped and enhanced the content of this book. Your willingness to contribute your knowledge and experience was crucial to its growth. I am grateful to the innumerable entrepreneurs and individuals with whom I have had the opportunity to work and learn. Your experiences, obstacles, and successes have provided me with priceless insights and a thorough comprehension of the entrepreneurial voyage. Your tenacity and resolve have served as a constant reminder of the boundless potential that resides within each of us.

I am grateful to editors, proofreaders, and designers for devoting their time and expertise to ensuring that this book achieves its maximum potential. Your attention to detail, professionalism, and dedication to excellence have significantly improved the outcome. I extend my deepest gratitude to my peers and coworkers who have provided me with encouragement, feedback, and words of wisdom. Your unwavering support and unwavering confidence in me have been a constant source of motivation and inspiration. I would like to express my sincere appreciation to those who have read this book. These pages have been written with the intention of motivating, empowering, and directing you, the reader, on your path to success. Your confidence and willingness to embark on this transformative journey are invaluable to me.

Once again, I am eternally grateful to everyone who has helped bring "Renew Your Mind for Success" to reality. May this book be a catalyst for positive change, personal development, and the actualization of your maximum potential.

With profound gratitude,
Tannizia Gasper

Foreword

Having served in leadership positions in both sacred and secular institutions for over forty years. I am quite familiar with the contours of corporate financial structures, systems, and practices as they function in developing countries like Guyana.

The entrepreneur in Tannizia Gasper writes through the lens of a wife, and mother. She does this through the labyrinth of uncertainty, insecurity, disillusionment, frustration, and fear. In her book, this emerging entrepreneur interacts with varying business theories and practical experiences rolling out in the process its central message on how to unlock the secrets of the mind.

The value of this book is not limited to the strategies, insights, and well-stocked toolbox. Rather, it challenges its readers to strive for transformational thinking.

RENEW YOUR MIND FOR SUCCESS reflects the author's faith, which is rooted in the biblical injunction found in Romans 12:2 NIV

"Do not conform to the patterns of the world, but be transformed by the renewing of your mind ..."

I recommend this book as an empowerment tool to young persons involved in business living and working within a developing context.

Dr. M. Raphael Massiah, Bishop

First Assembly of God /Wortmanville

CONTENTS

Introduction

To believe in something and not live it is dishonest. —
Mahatma Gandhi

Are you exhausted from feeling depleted by a business that consumes your energy? The very passion that once fueled your ambitions has become a double-edged sword due to seemingly insurmountable challenges and obstacles. Hope, which was once a guiding light, now seems like a distant memory, and the fractured remnants of your aspirations are strewn across the rubble of a life that has lost its luster.

The days of relationships based on mutual trust and benefit are long gone. The element of accord that once held partnerships together has dissolved, leaving a vacuum of broken promises and unrealized potential. Perhaps the financial upheaval's turbulent winds swept away your savings, or perhaps it was the persistent knocking on your door by creditors—a sobering reminder of the impending debts. The agony is palpable, permeating your entire being and leaving you exhausted and disheartened. The weight of your circumstances feels suffocating, threatening to extinguish the remaining spark of hope within.

In spite of this gloom, a glimmer of hope exists: an opportunity to revitalize, to rise from the ashes of despair, and to reclaim your strength. "Renew Your Mind for Success" is a guiding light for this transformational journey to a proven path to a sustainable livelihood. It provides a map for navigating treacherous terrain, healing the wounds inflicted by adversity, and reigniting the inner fire. Within the pages of this book, you will discover the tools, strategies, and insights necessary to reconstruct your business, reignite your passion, and regain control of your destiny. We will navigate the labyrinth of our thoughts and beliefs chapter by chapter, discarding limiting paradigms and adopting a new perspective that paves the way for long-term success. We will unlock the secrets of our minds and find the keys to realizing our full potential under the guidance of best practices and seven fundamental principles for generating sustainable income and building long-term wealth. The principles are as follows: your vision must be clearly defined and understood; your income is proportional to the value you create; change is inevitable; you must be adaptable; the best strategy requires the best structure or system; the strength of your relationships affects the strength of your financial standing; and you must maintain a fresh perspective on your growth.

Now, take a deep breath, collect the shattered pieces of your aspirations, and join us on this transformative odyssey. The path ahead may be difficult, but within the depths of your suffering lies the spark that will ignite a better future. The time has come to cast off the shackles of hopelessness and embrace the inner strength that will renew your mind for lasting success. It is an invitation to rise above the chaos and create a new story—one of perseverance, development, and ultimate victory.

I have been immersed in the world of entrepreneurship for more than a decade, attentively observing the trials and tribulations of ambitious individuals in the microfinance industry. During this time, a recurring theme emerged, one that permeated numerous conversations and exchanges. Entrepreneurs, eager to expand their enterprises, pointed the finger at the banking system, accusing it of prejudice, harshness, and a refusal to provide the necessary funds. I observed entrepreneurs who, after receiving coveted financial backing, embarked on a path that initially appeared promising. However, as the months passed, their businesses began to disintegrate, deviating from the meticulously crafted business plans that once held such promise. It became clear that the challenge did not stem from external factors but rather from their very essence.

Through years of observing and analyzing these patterns, I came to a profound realization. It was not the banking system or external circumstances that determined their fate, but rather their perceptions, beliefs, and mentality. As I probed deeper into their stories and empathized with their propensity to attribute failure to external factors, I, too, understood the appeal of doing so. I write to you today from a place of understanding and relatability. As a keen observer and evaluator, my experiences have led me to recognize the inherent power of perception and faith in the entrepreneurial voyage. I have personally witnessed how a misaligned mindset can undermine even the most promising endeavors. I step forward as a trusted guide on this transformative path with a sense of duty and a burning desire to help. With a comprehensive understanding of the difficulties entrepreneurs confront and years of experience in the microfinance industry, I offer you not only theories and philosophies but also the practical knowledge I've gained from countless interactions with business owners. My credibility stems from my unwavering dedication to revealing the truth about entrepreneurial success. It is a commitment born from observing the struggles, setbacks, and triumphs of those who ventured to dream enormously. Numerous hours have been spent evaluating and analyzing the factors that truly drive business growth and personal satisfaction.

It is time to enter your zone of ingenuity, reignite your passion, and rebuild a successful business that reflects your vision. Invest in your personal and professional development by immersing yourself in the transformative teachings presented in this book. **The ability to revitalize your psyche for success is within your reach.**

CHAPTER 1

Unleash the Power Within: the Effects of Thoughts on Achievements

Accept no one's definition of your life, but define yourself.
—Harvey Fierstein

Learning objectives

This chapter will assist you in comprehending the following critical success factors:

> **LO1:** Acquire knowledge of the mind's potential and its effect on business success.
>
> **LO2:** Learn how your thoughts create your reality.
>
> **LO3:** Identify common mental barriers that may be limiting business success.

What if the key to increasing your income lies not in external forces but in your own mind? Imagine using your full mental capacity to achieve success in a company of exceptional distinction. The capacity of the mind is one of the most exciting and potent aspects of human existence. Thoughts, beliefs, and attitudes have a substantial impact on our lives, particularly our professional success. Please take note that conscious and subconscious minds are two distinct mind categories.

Mind's cognizant state

The conscious mind can be defined as the portion of the brain that is aware of the present environment, thoughts, emotions, and sensations. Our waking state is the portion of our mind that we are actively aware of and can regulate. The conscious mind is responsible for our perception of reality and our capacity to make decisions and perform actions based on that perception, as well as to solve problems and communicate. It is also responsible for our short-term memory, which allows us to retain information temporarily.

Despite the fact that the conscious mind is the portion of the mind that we are conscious of, it is essential to note that it is not the only aspect of our mental functioning. Both conscious and unconscious processes influence our thoughts, emotions, and behaviors, and it is the interaction between these various levels of the mind that shapes our experience of the world. It represents only a minor portion of our mental activity as a whole.

The mind's subconscious

The subconscious mind is responsible for the majority of our mental processes. The subconscious mind is the portion of the mind that functions beneath the threshold of conscious awareness and responsible for our instinctive thoughts, emotions, and behaviors, as well as our deeply held beliefs and values. Even when we are not consciously aware, the subconscious mind is always active, processing information and influencing our behavior. Additionally, it is in charge of shaping the associations and repeated experiences that form our learned responses to various stimuli.

One of the primary functions of the brain is to retain and process information not immediately accessible to conscious awareness. This data may include memories, emotions, and beliefs formed throughout our lives. Our subconscious mind can also filter and interpret sensory information to help us make sense of our environment. This part of the mind is believed to be the origin of our emotions, memories, intuition, and creativity. It is the portion of our mind that permits us to process information much more quickly than our conscious mind, which has a limited capacity to do so. It is responsible for our sincerely held beliefs and values, which can have a profound effect on our thoughts, feelings, and actions. Even when we are aware of them, it can be challenging to change these beliefs and values because they can come from our experiences, upbringing, culture, and other factors.

James Fraser: From Dyslexia to Success

James Fraser, a young boy from the close-knit community of Linden, confronted a unique challenge at an early age. Reading and writing were challenging for him because he struggled with dyslexia, a learning disorder. While his contemporaries effortlessly assimilated written language, James frequently confused letters and words. This learning obstacle appeared insurmountable and impeded his academic success.

James was blessed with a mother who was incredibly nurturing and profoundly concerned for his wellbeing. She refused to let dyslexia define him because she recognized his indomitable spirit and unwavering resolve to surmount any obstacle. She witnessed a child with aspirations of attaining greatness and positively impacting his community.

James developed an unexpected interest in entrepreneurship as he aged. This passion was ignited when his parents gave him oranges to sell as a child. He realized that owning a business would allow him to define his own success and create opportunities for others. After his father's death, he was inspired to establish a small grocery store after gaining experience assisting in the family liquor store.

Especially for someone with dyslexia, starting a business from the beginning presented daunting obstacles. Along the journey, James encountered numerous obstacles. Due to his dyslexia, he had difficulty managing inventory, writing labels, and handling financial documents. However, he refused to allow these obstacles to impede his advancement.

James accessed his inner fortitude with unwavering determination. To overcome his dyslexia in the business realm, he sought innovative solutions. He used speech-to-text software to assist with writing, collaborated with trusted family and colleagues on paperwork, and implemented technology to streamline inventory management. James realized that success required flexibility and a willingness to seek assistance when necessary.

James' grocery store, aptly titled "James & Sons," flourished over time. James's store became a household name in the Linden community, not only for the quality of its products but also for the welcoming atmosphere he cultivated. He greeted customers by name, listened to their experiences, and went above and beyond to ensure everyone felt valued. James' personal journey and dedication to community service earned him a place in the affections of those he served. Today, James & Sons is more than just a grocery store; it is a symbol of perseverance, resolve, and inner strength. The narrative of James Fraser has become an inspiration for many in Linden and beyond. Young children with dyslexia view him as a role model because they recognize that their learning differences do not determine their potential for success.

James continues to tap into his inner strength, pursuing continuous improvement and innovation. He actively supports dyslexia organizations and advocates for greater understanding and assistance for those with learning differences. James has not only built a flourishing business through his grocery store, but he has also created a community where everyone feels seen, heard, and valued.

The story of James Fraser serves as a reminder that embracing one's unique qualities and overcoming challenges with tenacity and determination leads to true success. His transformation from a dyslexic child to a community icon is a demonstration of the ability we all possess to shape our own destinies and have a positive impact on the world.

LO1: Thoughts Dictate Actions and Influence Success

Philosophers, scientists, and academics have been studying and exploring the mind for centuries. Today, we have a greater understanding of the mind's incredible capabilities and how to leverage its strength to achieve our goals and aspirations. It is one of the most intriguing and potent instruments known to man. It has the ability to create, imagine, and solve complex problems. The power of the mind is so extensive that it can change the world, from the creation of extraordinary inventions to the alteration of historical events. Let's discharge our tremendous inner strength.

The mind is capable of influencing our perceptions, actions, and beliefs. Our beliefs serve as a lens through which we view the world, influencing our thoughts, emotions, and behavior. For instance, if we believe we are capable of attaining a certain objective, we are more likely to take the necessary steps to do so. Alternatively, if we believe we are not good enough or capable enough to complete a task, we may not even attempt it or, if we do attempt it, give up soon.

Our thoughts also affect our actions. If you have a positive view of yourself and your abilities, you are more likely to pursue your objectives and take action. In contrast, negative beliefs may cause you to avoid challenges and opportunities.

Our perceptions of the world around us have an impact on it. If you have negative beliefs, for instance, you may perceive a situation to be worse than it actually is. Conversely, if you have positive thoughts, you may perceive a situation to be more superior than it actually is.

The mind is crucial to our capacity to manage stress and surmount obstacles. When confronted with challenging situations, our thoughts and beliefs can either help us cope or exacerbate our stress level. For instance, if we view a difficult circumstance as an opportunity for development and learning, we are more likely to feel empowered and motivated to find solutions. There are people who have conquered addiction, chronic pain, and other conditions by altering their perspective and focusing on positive outcomes. Others have been able to heal their bodies through the power of positive thinking and visualization, with some even claiming to have cured themselves of cancer or other severe illnesses. In contrast, if we perceive the same circumstance as a threat, we may feel overwhelmed and helpless.

Our mental health can also affect our physical well-being. Studies indicate that tension, anxiety, and other negative emotions can have a negative impact on our bodies, leading to increased inflammation, weakened immune function, and an increased risk of developing chronic diseases. By learning to manage our thoughts and emotions, we can reduce our risk for these health problems and enhance our overall well-being.

Maximize Business Potential through Mindset

External factors like market trends, products, and strategies are not the only determinants of success. While these factors unquestionably play a significant role, there is a potent yet frequently disregarded factor that can make all the difference in unlocking a company's true potential: attitude. The maximization of business potential through mindset is a concept that explores the impact of our thoughts, beliefs, and attitudes on our entrepreneurial journey. Entrepreneurs and business professionals can propel themselves to greater success, surmount obstacles, and achieve extraordinary results by understanding and utilizing the power of mindset.

Fundamentally, mindset refers to the lens through which we perceive and interpret our surroundings. It includes our thoughts, beliefs, and attitudes and influences our perspectives, choices, and actions. While external circumstances unquestionably impact our business endeavors, it is ultimately our perspective that determines how we navigate and respond to those circumstances. A renewed and growth-oriented perspective enables us to view obstacles as opportunities, setbacks as learning opportunities, and failures as stepping stones to success. A fixed and limiting mindset, on the other hand, can impede progress, foster self-doubt, and impede innovation.

To maximize business potential through mindset, we must consciously alter the way we think about and approach business endeavors. It requires recognizing and challenging our limiting beliefs, cultivating a mindset of possibility and abundance, and developing methods for overcoming mental obstacles. Entrepreneurs can unlock their inherent potential and adopt a proactive approach to personal and professional development by adopting a growth mindset. They become resistant to obstacles, adaptable to shifting market conditions, and receptive to new ideas and opportunities.

Attitude is one way in which our beliefs can influence our business success. Your outlook on yourself, your team, and your business can determine your level of success. You will be more motivated to work diligently, take risks, and overcome obstacles if you have a positive attitude. Conversely, a negative attitude can hold you back, demotivate your team, and result in lost opportunities. Imagine, that two business proprietors each experience a setback in their respective enterprises. The first owner has a pessimistic outlook and implies that the setback spells the end of their company. The second proprietor is optimistic and views the setback as an opportunity to grow and learn. The second owner is more likely to surmount the setback, gain insight from the experience, and emerge from the situation stronger.

Mindset is another way in which our thoughts can influence business success. A growth mindset, which is the belief that skills and abilities can be developed through hard work and perseverance, can contribute to greater achievement. Individuals with a growth mindset are more likely to take risks, learn from their errors, and view obstacles as opportunities for personal development. Consider two entrepreneurs who are unveiling a new product as an example. The first entrepreneur has a fixed mindset and believes that their success is the result of their innate intellect and talent. If the product does not take off immediately, they may abandon it and conclude that they lack the qualities necessary for success. The second entrepreneur has a development mindset and believes that hard work and perseverance are the foundations of success. If the product does not take off immediately, the company may pivot, learn from consumer feedback, and iterate until success is achieved.

Our thoughts can elicit emotions that affect our success. If we have persistently negative thoughts about a situation, we may experience anxiety or tension, which can influence our actions and behavior. Conversely, if we think positively, we may feel more confident and motivated, which can result in positive actions and outcomes.

The influence of mindset transcends individual performance. It influences the collective mindset of teams and employees and permeates the organizational culture. When leaders prioritize and cultivate a renewed and growth-oriented mentality within their organizations, they foster an atmosphere of innovation, collaboration, and continuous improvement. In turn, this creates a solid foundation for maximizing business potential, as employees are empowered to bring their best selves to work, to think creatively, and to contribute to the company's overall success.

Throughout this voyage of maximizing business potential through mindset, individuals and organizations acquire the tools and insights necessary to overcome obstacles, transform obstacles into opportunities, and achieve remarkable results. Entrepreneurs and business professionals embark on a path to unlocking their full potential and achieving enduring success by recognizing the power of mindset and consciously cultivating a refreshed, growth-oriented perspective

LO2: The Creative Power of Thoughts

Our thoughts possess immense and frequently underappreciated power. Each person has the power to influence his or her own reality through the thoughts he or she chooses to entertain and cultivate. Through our beliefs, we construct our perception of the world, shape our actions, and ultimately determine our fate. This section will examine the profound relationship between thoughts and reality, demonstrating how our thoughts have the capacity to shape and mold the world we experience.

Our perceptions are the fundamental components of our reality. What we concentrate on mentally has the potential to manifest physically. Our thoughts serve as a blueprint for our beliefs, attitudes, and subsequent actions. Positive, constructive thoughts have the power to attract positivity and success, whereas negative thoughts can lead to self-doubt and a narrow view of possibilities.

The strength of belief structures

The robustness of belief structures is a fundamental aspect of human thought and has a significant impact on our perceptions, decisions, and actions. Belief structure refers to an individual's interconnected network of beliefs, values, and assumptions that serve as the basis for their perspective on the world. This complex system influences how we interpret information, form opinions, and evaluate our surroundings. The robustness of belief structure refers to the durability, coherence, and resilience of these underlying beliefs, which can have a significant effect on our resilience in the face of challenges, our ability to adapt to new information, and our capacity for critical thought. Understanding the robustness of belief structures provides valuable insights into the mechanisms underlying human belief systems and offers a means of fostering intellectual development, effective communication, and an open mind.

Our beliefs, which determine our perception of reality, are intricately intertwined with our thoughts. Through the lens of our beliefs, we interpret and make sense of the world. If we hold limiting beliefs that undermine our abilities or success potential, we impose a barrier on ourselves. In contrast, empowering beliefs can propel us toward accomplishments beyond our wildest dreams. By scrutinizing and challenging our beliefs consciously, we can reframe our thoughts and create new opportunities.

Putting thoughts into practice

Implementing our thoughts is not simply a theoretical exercise; it is the key to unleashing our true potential and creating the reality we desire. By comprehending the profound connection between our thoughts and our actual experiences, we gain the ability to influence our perception, our beliefs, and ultimately the world we inhabit.

Our thoughts are the builders of our reality. They form the basis upon which our actions are constructed. Positive and optimistic thoughts become the catalyst behind our desires and actions, guiding us towards our goals. Negative thoughts, in contrast, can be self-limiting, impede our progress and prevent us from reaching our maximum potential.

Before we can harness the transformative power of our beliefs, we must acknowledge their impact on our lives. By becoming aware of our dominant thoughts, we can gain insight into their influence on our behaviors and emotions. Self-awareness enables us to recognize unproductive thought patterns and replace them with more beneficial ones.

Once we recognize the power of our beliefs, we can intentionally cultivate a mindset that supports our goals. By adopting a positive outlook and cultivating beliefs that are congruent with our goals, we create an interior environment that is conducive to growth and success.

However, mere thought is insufficient. To materialize our visions, we must take deliberate actions consistent with those thoughts and convictions. We bring our aspirations to fruition by exerting consistent effort and devoting ourselves. Each action we take is a launching pad toward the achievement of our goals.

As we progress along this path of aligning our thoughts and actions, we begin to perceive a symbiotic relationship between the two. This synergy strengthens our resolve, enhances our confidence, and attracts opportunities that propel us even further. In essence, we become the architects of our own destinies, sculpting them in accordance with our intentions.

LO3: Common Barriers that Limit Success

Success in the dynamic business environment requires more than a superior product or service. Owners of businesses must navigate a number of complex obstacles, such as competition, market volatility, and shifting consumer preferences. However, the greatest obstacles are frequently rooted in our own beliefs and attitudes. This section will examine mental barriers such as fear of failure, self-doubt, perfectionism, lack of focus, and resistance to change, as well as their impact on business success and strategies for overcoming them. By identifying and addressing these obstacles, business leaders can maximize their success and realize their maximum potential.

Dread of failing

Fear of failure is a common and natural human emotion that prevents people from reaching their maximum potential. Anxiety, self-doubt, and even melancholy are frequently present along with this. Nevertheless, it is essential to acknowledge that failure is an inevitable part of life and can be a valuable learning experience.

The mental capacity of a person is crucial to overcoming their dread of failure. It is up to us to determine whether our thoughts and beliefs empower or limit us. We are more likely to avoid taking risks and pursuing our objectives, for instance, if we believe that failure is something to be ashamed of or that it defines us as individuals. In contrast, we can develop resilience and perseverance if we perceive failure as an opportunity to learn and grow.

Self-Doubt

All individuals experience self-doubt at some stage in their lives. It is the feeling that you are inadequate, that you lack the skills or abilities necessary to succeed in your endeavors. Self-doubt is especially hazardous in the business world, where success frequently requires confidence, risk-taking, and a willingness to learn from mistakes. They may miss out on opportunities or fall short of their objectives if they are constantly doubting themselves or believing that they lack the skills necessary for success.

Self-doubt can manifest in a variety of ways, from challenging your abilities to feeling like a fraud in your position. Lack of experience or knowledge, unfavorable comments from others, or simply comparing oneself to others in the same field can all be contributing factors. Regardless of its source, self-doubt can be extremely paralyzing, leading to procrastination, avoidance, and even the abandonment of one's objectives.

Perfectionism

Perfectionism is a personality trait characterized by establishing excessively high standards for oneself and seeking perfection in all endeavors. While striving for excellence can lead to success in a variety of spheres of life, including business, perfectionism frequently results in negative consequences.

Perfectionists have a tendency to be overly critical of their own work, resulting in a dread of failure that can impede advancement and productivity. This can manifest itself in a variety of ways in the business world, including excessive revision and delays in the introduction of a product or service, a lack of delegation and micromanagement of team members, and a tendency to overwork oneself. These manifestations may result in burnout.

A business owner may spend months perfecting a product before releasing it to the market, but by the time the product is released, the market has changed and the product is no longer pertinent. Alternatively, a perfectionist may be incapable of delegating duties to team members, resulting in an inability to effectively scale their business. Moreover, a perfectionist may work long hours and prioritize work over health, resulting in fatigue and health problems that can have long-term negative effects on their business.

It is essential to note, however, that not all perfectionism is detrimental. Certain industries, including healthcare and aviation, require precision in order to ensure safety and prevent errors. In addition, setting high standards for oneself can result in personal growth and development if it is balanced with a realistic comprehension of one's limitations and a willingness to learn from one's mistakes.

Absence of focus

In the dynamic business environment of today, a lack of concentration can be a significant barrier to success. A lack of focus occurs when individuals lack a clear comprehension of their objectives, resulting in a lack of direction and purpose. This issue can have a substantial impact on the success of a business because it can lead to ignored opportunities, wasted resources, and poor decision-making.

A startup company that fails to define a distinct business model or target market is an instance in which a lack of focus can negatively affect business success. Without a clear understanding of their customers and value proposition, the company may have difficulty attracting and retaining customers, resulting in low revenue and, eventually, failure. Similarly, a lack of focus on product development can result in the creation of products that do not meet market demands, leading to poor sales and a lack of profitability.

Resistance to Change

Adaptation is inevitable in today's dynamic business environment. To remain competitive, entrepreneurs must adapt to new technologies, trends, and market adjustments. Change can be difficult for some business proprietors, who may oppose new initiatives, processes, or strategies. This resistance to change can have substantial effects on a company's success.

Change resistance is the negative response of employees or constituents to organizational change initiatives. It is a natural reaction because it disrupts individuals' established patterns, routines, and expectations. Change resistance can take many forms, including skepticism, anxiety, apathy, and even active opposition. Fear of the unknown, lack of trust in management, a perceived loss of power or status, and concerns regarding personal or group interests are common causes of resistance to change.

There are numerous examples of change resistance in business environments. The adoption of new technologies, such as digital platforms or automation tools, is one of the most prevalent. Some employees may be resistant to using new software or equipment due to a lack of familiarity with the technology or a predilection for conventional procedures. A factory worker, for instance, may oppose the use of a new robotic arm for production because it may reduce the need for manual labor or necessitate retraining. Organizational restructuring, such as mergers and acquisitions, is another example. Due to uncertainty regarding their employment security, roles, and team dynamics, employees may resist such changes. They may also oppose cultural changes, such as new performance evaluation systems or leadership styles, that they perceive as unjust or biased.

How can you change your perspective to be more successful?

To attain financial success, you can change your mindset using a variety of resources. I will describe five instruments that can be utilized regardless of where you are in your personal or professional life.

Positive affirmations are statements that reflect a positive frame of mind and are repeated frequently. By consistently repeating positive affirmations, you can begin to reprogram your subconscious and alter your beliefs to be more positive and empowering. For instance, you could repeat affirmations such as "I am worthy of financial success" or "I have the skills and abilities to achieve my financial goals."

Visualization is a technique in which you imagine yourself accomplishing your financial objectives in great detail, using all of your senses to make the experience as real as possible. Visualization can help you create a vivid mental image of your desired outcomes, making them seem more attainable and boosting your motivation to achieve them.

Practicing gratitude is a potent method for cultivating a positive attitude. By focusing on what you're grateful for, you can shift your attention away from negative thoughts and emotions and toward a more positive and abundant mindset. You can practice gratitude by writing down three things you are grateful for each day or by spending a few minutes each day reflecting on what you are grateful for.

Language associated with a growth mindset: The language you use can also have a significant impact on your mindset. Using growth-oriented language, such as "I can learn from this experience" or "I am capable of achieving my goals," can help you adopt a growth-oriented and optimistic frame of mind.

Setting goals can help you focus your attention and energy on attaining your desired outcomes. By setting SMART (specific, measurable, attainable, relevant, and time-bound) goals, you can construct a road map to financial success and track your progress along the way.

We embark on a path of self-discovery and personal empowerment if we can embrace Harvey Fierstein's advice to define ourselves rather than allowing others to do so. We investigated the capacity of the mind and its extraordinary impact on business success. By understanding the power of our thoughts, we open ourselves to a universe of possibilities. The key to unlocking our potential and attaining extraordinary results in our professional endeavors is recognizing that our thoughts determine our reality.

We investigated the notion that our thoughts create our reality in greater depth. This emphasizes the significance of cultivating a positive mindset and thinking in line with our intended outcomes. We can manifest our goals and aspirations into reality by harnessing the power of positive thinking and visualizing success. We examined the prevalent mental obstacles that frequently impede business success. These barriers function as impediments, preventing us from advancing and reaching our full potential. Awareness of these obstacles paves the way for their eventual elimination, allowing us to surmount them and propel ourselves to success. Now that we are equipped with this knowledge, we can unleash our inner strength and embark on a remarkable voyage towards achieving our business objectives. Realizing that how we define ourselves and the beliefs we choose to cultivate are the foundation of success

It is impossible to overstate the significance of mindset in attaining financial success. The way you think affects how you perceive money, your spending habits, and your ability to save and invest. By understanding your current money mindset, you can identify any limiting beliefs or negative patterns that impede financial growth. The knowledge gained can facilitate a change in your money mindset and the development of positive habits that support your financial objectives. So, let's investigate your current money mindset.

Activity: Realistic Evaluation

Instruction:

a. Take approximately twenty minutes of uninterrupted time to consider your current business-related thoughts and beliefs.

b. Document any negative or limiting beliefs that you may have identified.

c. Consider Harvey Fierstein's admonition to *Accept no one's definition of your life, but define yourself* and identify any specific adjustments you can make to unleash your inner power and improve your business success.

d. Make a decision to take action.

CHAPTER 2

Break the Money Mold: Unlock Your Wealth Mindset

The mind is an incredible tool. What you believe becomes reality —**Tannizia Gasper**

Learning objectives

This chapter will help you understand the following factors that are critical to unlocking your wealth mindset:

LO1: Learn the concept of "money mold" and how it limits your financial potential

LO2: Identify your personal money mold and your negative thought patterns that hinder your financial success.

LO3: Learn how to break the mold and unlock your wealth mindset.

Is your business struggling to achieve the financial success you envision? Then it's time to shatter the limiting beliefs that are holding you back and unleash your true potential for sustainable income. In the same way that a physical mold shapes the form and structure of the material it develops on, our money mold shapes the way we think about money and ultimately the financial outcomes we achieve.

LO1: Money Mold

Our upbringing, the messages we've received from society, and our own ideas and beliefs about success and wealth all have an impact on how we interact with money. These influences can result in what is commonly referred to as a "money mold," a set of profoundly ingrained attitudes and behaviors regarding money that can either facilitate or impede our financial success. If you grew up hearing messages such as "money doesn't grow on trees," "money is the root of all evil," or "money will make you walk funny," you may have developed a negative money mold that prevents you from pursuing wealth and financial success.

How your thoughts shape your wealth potential

It has been said that we become what we think about. Your financial success as an entrepreneur depends not only on your business creativity but also on your personal financial perspective. To achieve financial success as an entrepreneur, it is crucial to recognize your personal money mold and any negative thought patterns that may be impeding your progress. Understanding your money personality is crucial, as it can affect the way you make financial decisions and your financial success. For instance, if you were raised in a family where money was a scarce resource, you may have developed a scarcity mentality and be hesitant to invest in your business or take financial risks.

Negative thought patterns can also have a big impact on financial success. These patterns are limiting beliefs that can prevent you from reaching your financial objectives. Negative thought patterns include beliefs such as "I'm not good enough to be successful" or "I'll never be able to make enough money". These negative thought patterns may manifest in your business and prevent you from taking the necessary steps to achieve financial success.

Awareness is the first step to inner transformation and building resilience. It helps you determine how your thoughts, emotions, and actions align with your internal standards—how you perceive yourself and how others perceive you. Consider the money-related messages you received as a child, the financial decisions you have made in the past, and any fears or doubts you have about your capacity to achieve financial success. When you identify your family's money-related beliefs and values, you will be able to assess their influence on your own beliefs.

Below are some ways in which these variables can influence your perspective on money:

Your personal financial experiences as a child can also influence your financial beliefs. If your family has experienced financial hardship, for instance, you may regard money as a source of drama and stress. Our childhood financial experiences can also influence our money beliefs. If our family has encountered financial difficulties, you may view money as a source of drama and stress.

Your socioeconomic status as a child can also have an impact on your financial beliefs. For instance, if you grew up in a low-income family, you may have learned to be resourceful and put necessities ahead of wants.

The cultural norms surrounding money can also influence your beliefs and attitudes. Some cultures place a high value on material prosperity, while others place a lower value on it.

Education and media: The messages about money that you receive through education and media can also influence your beliefs. For instance, you may adopt similar values if you are exposed to media messages that glorify material affluence.

Fear of taking risks: Investing and entrepreneurship frequently involve taking risks, which can be frightening for some individuals. You may miss out on opportunities for financial growth and success if you are too risk-averse.

Limiting beliefs and negative self-talk: Your thoughts and beliefs about money can have an impact on your financial decisions and outcomes. If you have negative thoughts or limiting beliefs about money, such as "I'll never be rich" or "Money is the root of all evil," you may sabotage your financial success and restrict your potential.

Financial illiteracy: If you lack knowledge and comprehension of personal finance, investing, and other financial concepts, you may make poor financial decisions that can limit your wealth creation and growth potential. If you are overspending and accruing debt, you are likely limiting your financial potential by paying interest and fees rather than investing in your future.

Absence of a financial plan: Without a clear financial plan and objectives, you may lack direction and purpose in your financial decisions, limiting your long-term financial success potential.

Activity:

a. Take a piece of paper and divide it into two columns.

b. In the first column, write down your earliest money memories. These could be experiences related to money such as receiving an allowance, going shopping with your parents, or hearing them talk about money. Write down as many memories as you can recall.

c. In the second column, write down the beliefs or attitudes about money that you developed as a result of these experiences. For example, if your earliest memory of money was your parents arguing about money, you may have developed a belief that money causes stress and conflict.

d. Take thirty minutes to reflect on your list and consider how your earliest money experiences have influenced your current money mindset. Do you still hold on to any of these beliefs? Do they serve you well or hold you back from achieving financial success?

Our upbringing and cultural heritage can have a substantial effect on our beliefs and attitudes regarding money. Our family's outlook and values encourage this. For example, if our parents were parsimonious and stressed the significance of saving, we may adopt similar values. Our childhood financial experiences can also influence our financial beliefs. If our family has encountered financial difficulties, you may view money as a source of drama and stress.

LO2: Unmasking your Money Mold

Our money blueprints stem from our beliefs and thought patterns and have a significant impact on our financial success. These preconceived notions are the consequences of societal norms, individual experiences, and inherited beliefs. In this section, we will discuss the significance of recognizing our personal money molds and the negative thought patterns that impede our financial success. By acknowledging and addressing these obstacles, we can take proactive measures toward achieving greater financial security.

Understanding the Money Mold

The money mold represents the framework of our financial beliefs and attitudes. It consists of inherited perspectives, cultural influences, and personal experiences that shape our relationship with money. These molds operate on a subliminal level, influencing our financial decisions and behaviors without our awareness.

The Influence of Unhealthy Thought Patterns

Within the money paradigm, negative thought patterns present substantial barriers to financial success. These patterns may include a dreaded feeling of scarcity, self-limiting beliefs, and an emphasis on immediate gratification as opposed to long-term objectives. The belief that money is limited and difficult to acquire is the root cause of the fear of scarcity. This way of thinking can result in a constant state of anxiety and prevent individuals from taking calculated risks or investigating opportunities that may lead to financial growth.

Next, self-limiting beliefs are formidable impediments to financial success. These beliefs may manifest as feelings of unworthiness, a lack of confidence in one's ability to acquire or manage money, or the notion that financial success is reserved for an elite few. These thought patterns create self-imposed barriers that prevent individuals from pursuing their maximum potential and impede their ability to seize lucrative opportunities.

Lastly, the enticement of instant gratification can be detrimental to long-term financial success. A cycle of debt, limited savings, and missed opportunities for wealth accumulation is the result of succumbing to impulsive spending and prioritizing immediate pleasures over responsible financial management.

Recognizing Your Money Mold and Negative Thinking Patterns

The process of self-discovery could reveal our deeply ingrained money habits and negative thought patterns. Some individuals may have a mindset of scarcity, characterized by a constant fear that there will never be enough money, which prevents them from investing or taking financial risks. Others may have a profoundly ingrained belief that they are not deserving of financial success, resulting in subconscious self-sabotage when opportunities for prosperity arise. These patterns may also manifest as guilt or discomfort regarding money, making it difficult to accumulate wealth or even effectively manage it. It begins by analyzing our upbringing, cultural influences, and early financial experiences.

Recognizing these money molds and negative thought patterns is not about placing responsibility on ourselves or others; rather, it is about recognizing their existence so that we can begin the process of escaping their constraints. With awareness comes the potential for change and development. Once identified, these limiting beliefs can be challenged and replaced with more empowering thoughts and attitudes regarding money. This transformation can provide us with new opportunities for financial success and abundance. Adopting a positive money mindset and cultivating a healthy relationship with money can pave the way to attaining our financial objectives and ensuring a prosperous future.

Confronting limiting Money Belief

Confronting our limiting money beliefs is a process of transformation that requires commitment and perseverance. Once these beliefs and thought patterns have been identified, it is imperative to take proactive measures to overcome them and cultivate financial success. Awareness is the first and most crucial stage. By becoming aware of our negative thought patterns and recognizing their impact on our financial decisions, we can begin to break free from their control. This self-awareness enables us to challenge these limiting beliefs whenever they arise and replace them with more positive and empowering ones.

Education is essential to this course of action. The acquisition of financial knowledge and comprehension of sound money management principles equips us with the tools necessary to make informed decisions and navigate the complexities of personal finance competently. As our financial knowledge increases, we gain confidence in managing our finances and dispel the concerns that impede our progress.

A solid support system can also make a substantial difference. When we surround ourselves with people who share a positive financial outlook, we can gain inspiration, motivation, and valuable insights. Engaging in conversations with like-minded individuals can assist us in altering our perspective and achieving our financial objectives.

In addition, regularly affirming positive beliefs and reframing negative thoughts is a highly effective practice. By reiterating financial-related affirmations, we can reprogram our subconscious minds and replace limiting beliefs with empowering ones. This procedure requires perseverance and self-awareness, but the benefits are well worth the effort.

In summary, identifying our money molds and overcoming negative thought patterns are essential steps to achieving greater financial success. We can transform our relationship with money and pave the way for long-term financial security and success through awareness, education, support, and positive affirmations. Adopting these practices not only improves our financial well-being but also our perspective and outlook on life as a whole.

LO3: The Art of Reframing Your Money Perspective

Entrepreneurs recognize that the road to financial success is paved with challenges and obstacles that call for a specialized skill set and a resilient mindset. Our money mindset is one of the most essential factors in achieving success. Our money-related beliefs, attitudes, and behaviors have a significant impact on our ability to generate wealth and financial abundance. This section examines the concept of reframing a limiting money mindset and provides practical tools and activities to help business owners who are struggling to break out of their money molds and unlock their wealth mindset.

What does it mean to alter your money mindset?

Would you believe me if I told you that you have the ability to realize your complete financial potential if you simply alter your money mindset? Reframing is a powerful technique that enables you to change how you perceive and think about money, resulting in a more positive and empowered relationship with your finances. This allows us to consider our beliefs and attitudes regarding money, such as whether we perceive it as a source of stress or a tool for achieving our goals. Consider your financial routines and behaviors, such as how you spend, invest, and manage your money.

Practical tools for reframing limiting money mindset

Identifying Limiting Beliefs

To begin the journey of reframing your money perspective, you must identify your limiting money beliefs. Engage in journaling, reflection, or working with a coach to explore your negative money-related thoughts and beliefs. Put these beliefs on paper and counter them with positive affirmations or more empowering beliefs.

Here is an illustration:

Negative Belief	Positive Affirmation
I wasn't born with a gold spoon.	I have the ability to create wealth and abundance in my life.
I'm not good with money.	I am capable of managing my money and making smart financial decisions.
There's never enough money.	I have an abundance of resources available to me.

Remember the principle: *You will eat the fruit of your mouth.*

Therefore, it is important to speak with intention, kindness, and mindfulness.

Cultivating Gratitude

Practicing gratitude is an effective method for altering one's financial outlook. Understand the relationship between your mind and body, as well as the transformative effects of gratitude on your mental and physical health. Activities such as gratitude journals, gratitude meditation, and appreciation letters can be used to cultivate gratitude. Each day, reflect on the things for which you are grateful, write them down, or share them with others. This practice helps you shift from a perspective of scarcity to one of abundance, thereby alleviating tension, anxiety, and depression.

Creating a Budget and Tracking Spending

Developing financial awareness is essential for changing one's money perspective. Create a budget and monitor your spending to develop financial awareness. This method identifies areas of squandering and prioritizes expenses in accordance with your values and objectives. By actively administering your finances, you assume financial control.

Self-Education on Personal Finance and Investing

Educate yourself on personal finance and investing to empower yourself. The greater your knowledge, the better equipped you will be to make prudent financial decisions. Participate in the study of personal finance, investing, and wealth creation by perusing books, listening to podcasts, or taking courses. By increasing your financial knowledge, you will gain self-assurance and make prudent financial decisions.

Taking Reasonable Risks

Taking calculated risks is frequently required to overcome a limiting money mindset. Evaluate investment opportunities, launch a new business, or pursue alternative career paths. Evaluate the risks and benefits associated with each opportunity and align them with your objectives and values. You must courageously leave your comfort zone and embrace the possibility of substantial financial rewards.

Being in a positive environment

Your social circle has a big impact on your financial outlook. Surround yourself with peers, mentors, and community groups that support your financial objectives. Seek out those who provide encouragement, sound advice, and inspiration. Collaborate with and learn from individuals who share your financial success goals.

Reframing your perspective on money is a process that requires patience, practice, and perseverance. By incorporating practical tools and activities into your daily routine, you can gradually adopt an abundance mindset and realize your maximum financial potential. Remember that the first step is typically the most difficult, and celebrate your accomplishments along the way. On the path to financial achievement, you must seize opportunities, act decisively, and never give up.

The chapter highlights the power of the mind and the effect of our beliefs on the formation of our reality. We emphasize the notion that our beliefs ultimately shape our experiences. Understanding this concept is essential for improving our financial situation.

The "money mold" concept was introduced. This refers to the internalized beliefs, attitudes, and behaviors regarding money that we have developed over the course of our lives. By perpetuating negative thought patterns and erecting self-imposed obstacles, these stereotypes frequently limit our financial potential. By investigating and comprehending the money mold, we can gain insight into our current financial situation and identify areas for growth and change.

The reader is then guided through the process of determining his or her own personal financial profile. We emphasize the significance of self-reflection, introspection, and awareness of one's money-related thoughts, beliefs, and actions. By identifying and comprehending the negative thought patterns that inhibit financial success, individuals can begin to challenge and reframe these patterns.

We provide practical strategies and techniques to break the mold and unleash the wealth mentality. Among these are reframing limiting beliefs, replacing negative thoughts with positive affirmations, and cultivating an abundance and opportunity mindset. In appreciating what one already has and in attracting more abundance into one's life, we emphasize the power of gratitude.

Throughout the chapter, action and implementation are emphasized. Breaking the money paradigm is not merely a mental exercise; it requires deliberate action towards transformation. We encourage readers to develop healthy financial habits, set objectives that align with their vision, and pursue personal finance growth and learning on a consistent basis.

The reader will have gained a thorough comprehension of the money mold, its impact on their financial potential, and the necessity of identifying and challenging negative thought patterns. They will have learned actionable strategies to break free of the status quo and cultivate a wealth mindset that enables them to reach their financial objectives.

Activity: Breaking Free from Limiting Beliefs: Identifying Your Personal Money Mold

Objective: To help struggling business owners identify their personal money molds and negative thought patterns that hinder their financial success.

General Instructions:

Mind mapping is an effective technique that takes advantage of the brain's inherent ability to organize information through association and visualization. It promotes creative thought because it allows ideas to flow freely, unrestricted by linear thought or fixed outlines. It also improves information retention and understanding because the visual representation facilitates memory recall.

Mind Mapping:

a. Divide a sheet of paper or whiteboard into two sections labeled "Money Mold" and "Negative Thought Patterns."

b. Write down any beliefs or thought patterns about money that you feel may be hindering your financial success.

c. Consider and think about any fears, self-doubts, scarcity mindsets, or other negative beliefs you may hold.

d. Try to remember any personal experiences related to these beliefs and how they made you feel.

Reflection and reframing:

a. Critically analyze the identified money molds and negative thought patterns.

b. Make a list of what these beliefs and thought patterns have cost you.

c. Consider alternative perspectives or beliefs that could counteract these limiting beliefs.

Action Planning:

a. Create an action plan to address those identified money molds and negative thought patterns.

b. Write down specific steps to take to break free from these limitations and cultivate a more positive and empowering mindset.

c. Remember to set realistic goals and establish a timeline for implementing these action plans.

Conclusion:

Continue to explore and challenge those money molds and negative thought patterns, as there is a need for growth and long-term financial success.

CHAPTER 3

Seeing is Achieving:
A Blueprint for Transformative
Goal Setting

"The future belongs to those who believe in the beauty of their dreams." **—Eleanor Roosevelt**

Learning objectives

This chapter will help you understand the following factors that are critical to unlocking your wealth mindset:

LO1: Learn the principles of visualization and goal setting and how they can transform your thinking and build sustainable income.

LO2: Gain Knowledge on techniques for implementing visualization and goal-setting in your daily routine.

LO3: Learn the importance of staying focused on goals and maintaining a positive outlook.

As a child, I used to imagine and act like my favorite superheroes, Lois and Clark. Superman was powerful, fearless, and always there to save the day. The feeling of strength, fulfillment, and being special made me believe that anything was possible. Little did I know that this power of imagination, or what some would call daydreaming, was actually visualization.

Visualization is the process of creating a mental image of what we want to achieve or become. It is the first step in making our dreams a reality. As we visualize our goals, we create a mental image that allows us to feel a certain way. It's the feeling of already having achieved our goals that keeps us motivated and on track.

As I grew older, I realized that visualization is not just a childhood pastime but a powerful tool for success. By visualizing my goals and setting clear intentions, I was able to achieve things that I once thought were impossible. It allowed me to tap into my inner strength and resilience and overcome any obstacles that came my way.

Now, I want to share this powerful tool with others to help them achieve their dreams and create a life of abundance and success. With visualization, anything is possible. The key is to believe in ourselves and our ability to achieve our goals. So, let us take a moment to visualize our dreams, set our intentions, and take inspired actions towards making them a reality. The power is within us, and the possibilities are endless.

Visualization is not just a childhood pastime but a powerful tool for success. It has helped me tap into my inner strength and resilience, and it has also helped me overcome many obstacles that have come my way. It's the power of our imagination that allows us to create a vision of our desired future and the determination to make that vision a reality.

Now, whenever I see a child playing make-believe, I smile, knowing that they are tapping into their imagination and creating a vision of their future—a future where anything is possible—and that they are capable of achieving their dreams.

LOI: Transform Your Mindset, Transform Your Income

Imagine achieving your financial goals and building a sustainable income with ease. It's possible, with the powerful principles of visualization and goal setting, that you can transform your thinking and head towards success. When you learn how to use these principles effectively, you can set clear goals, create a detailed plan of action, and visualize yourself achieving success. Now that you know that you can use your imagination to create vivid pictures of yourself achieving your goals, you can now program your subconscious mind to work towards making those pictures a reality. When you visualize your success, you create a powerful positive energy that can help you stay motivated and focused on your goals.

Principle 1: Craft your Winning Vision

Are you ready to turn your dreams into a successful reality?

In the pursuit of transforming your thinking and generating a sustainable income, visioning is crucial to the realization of your ambitions. While visualization and goal-setting create the foundation for success, visioning takes these concepts one step further by integrating them into a comprehensive and executable plan. Creating a successful vision entails devising a well-thought-out strategy to transform that vision into a tangible reality, as opposed to simply visualizing the desired outcome. By combining the power of visualization with goal-setting, you create a clear and compelling mental image of your future success while outlining the specific objectives and actions necessary to achieve it. This process not only ignites your motivation and self-confidence but also gives you the ability to take purposeful steps toward your financial goals. Visioning allows you to align your values with your goals, remain focused on your path to success, and ultimately create a sustainable income that reflects your deepest desires and aspirations. This section will assist you on your visioning voyage by providing you with the tools and mindset you need to make your dreams a reality.

A vision is a statement that outlines a company's long-term aspirations and goals. It is a clear, concise description of the desired future state of the organization. A vision statement communicates the company's purpose, values, and priorities and serves as a guide for decision-making and strategic planning. A strong vision statement inspires and motivates employees, customers, and stakeholders and provides a framework for the company to achieve its goals and fulfill its mission. A well-crafted vision statement helps to establish a company's identity, reputation, and brand and sets the direction for future growth and success. Here is an example of my vision statement: *Empower entrepreneurs to achieve transformative change by instilling new, positive daily habits and mindset shifts that revolutionize their businesses.*

It's your turn; let's refine or define your vision statement based on what you have read. Take thirty minutes to look at your vision statement and consider the questions below.

Do you feel motivated by your vision statement?

Is it aligned with the company's purpose, values, and priorities?

Is it clear and concise enough to communicate your desired future state and guide your decision-making?

This will help ensure your vision is on the path to success and impact.

Principle 2: Define your goals

If visualization is to be effective, we must know the answer to the golden question: What do you want to achieve? Do you want to double your current income? Buy a house? Retire early? Once you have a clear idea of what you want, you can start to visualize yourself achieving those goals. Imagine yourself already in possession of your desired outcome. What does it look like? How does it feel? What are you doing? Who is with you? The more details you can imagine, the more real your visualization becomes.

Visualization can help you overcome obstacles and stay focused on your goals. When you encounter challenges or setbacks, you can use your mental images to remind yourself of why you are working so hard. By keeping your goals in mind, you can stay motivated and continue to make progress towards achieving them.

Goal setting

Visioning entails goal-setting, planning, and taking action in order to realize the envisioned future. It entails establishing specific goals, outlining the actions required to achieve them, and developing a plan for progress. Visioneering is the practice of combining the power of visualization with practical action in order to effectively manifest one's aspirations.

Goal setting is a critical process that translates a business's vision into specific, measurable performance targets. To ensure success, goals must be SMART, both short and long-term, and challenge the team to perform at its full potential. However, it's essential to distinguish between strategic and financial goals. While strategic objectives help position the business for long-term success and competitive advantage, financial goals ensure the long-term profitability and health of the company. A balanced approach that integrates both strategic and financial goals is essential for holistic business growth that aligns with the overall business model. As Peter Drucker once said, "What gets measured gets managed." So, setting effective goals is the key to success.

A clearly outlined vision and strategy are the components that give you direction. How do you set a goal? The fundamentals of goal-setting are to use the **SMART** framework.

SMART Framework

The fundamental of goal setting is to be SMART—an acronym for **s**pecific, **m**easurable, **a**chievable, **r**ealistic, and **t**ime-bound—what a goal should be.

S	Specific	Clearly define your goal	**What? Where? How?**
M	Measurable	Ensure that you can measure your progress.	**From and To**
A	Attainable	Set goals you can achieve that will stretch you.	**Possible?**
R	Realistic	Set a challenging target that is relevant to your business's development and growth.	**Difference made?**
T	Time Bound	Set a date for when your goals need to be achieved.	**When?**

What is a smart goal? Example of a smart goal:

A SMART objective is a well-defined and structured method for establishing and attaining goals. The SMART criteria assist individuals and organizations in formulating objectives that are specific, measurable, achievable, relevant, and time-bound.

Broad Goal Example: Set up an online Business.

Specific: I will sell handmade jewelry online. **Measurable:** I will aim to sell a minimum of twenty pieces per month. **Achievable:** I will set up my shop on Etsy.com. **Realistic:** Sell five pieces per week. **Time Bound:** I will sell one hundred by December 2023

Example: I Want To Increase My Profits

Specific: I will increase revenue while cutting down on expenditure. Moving to a more affordable premise that will cut my rent by 7% will reduce the operational costs.

Measurable: I will increase sales over the next 3 months by signing up 5 more potential clients.

Attainable: I will improve my current customer relationships and promote the business through referrals, networking, and social networks. This will help me find more leads and, therefore, lead to an increase in revenue for the business.

Realistic: Moving to a cheaper establishment will reduce the operational cost of my business and therefore give room for the growth of profits.

Time-bound: I will have increased my profit by the end of the coming three months.

To achieve your goals, you need to create a plan of action. This plan should include specific steps that you will take to achieve your goals, as well as timelines for when you will complete each step. By breaking your goals down into smaller, more achievable steps, you can stay focused on making progress and avoid becoming overwhelmed.

Activity: Visualization and Goal Setting

Objectives: Apply the principles of visualization and goal setting.

Instructions:

1. Define your financial goals. What do you want to achieve? Be specific and measurable.

2. Visualize yourself achieving your goals. Imagine yourself already in possession of your desired outcome. What does it look like? How does it feel? What are you doing? Who is with you?

3. Create a plan of action. Break your goals down into smaller, more achievable steps, and create a timeline for completing each step.

4. Stay focused on your goals. Use your mental images to remind yourself of why you are working so hard. Stay motivated by tracking your progress and celebrating your successes.

By using the principles of visualization and goal-setting, you can transform your thinking and build a sustainable income. By setting clear goals, creating a detailed plan of action, and visualizing yourself achieving success, you can stay motivated and focused on achieving your financial goals. So why wait? Start visualizing and goal setting today. Start building the life of your dreams!

LO2: Empowering Your Daily Routine

Visualization and goal setting are powerful tools that can transform your life and help you achieve success in various aspects. We will explore the importance of the techniques for implementing visualization and goal setting in our daily routine. By integrating these practices into our everyday lives, we can cultivate a focused mindset, stay motivated, and make steady progress towards our desired outcomes.

Define Clear and Specific Goals

Setting clear and specific goals is the first step towards implementing visualization and goal-setting in your daily routine. By defining what you want to achieve, you create a sense of direction and purpose. For example, if your goal is to expand your business online, you can visualize yourself managing a thriving e-commerce store, serving satisfied customers, and enjoying financial freedom. This mental image serves as a guiding force and keeps you motivated on a daily basis.

Creating Vision Board

Visual aids can be powerful tools for manifestation. One technique for implementing visualization into your daily routine is to create a vision board. A vision board is a collage of images, words, and symbols that represent your goals and aspirations. By placing it in a prominent place in your living room or workspace, you constantly expose yourself to visual reminders of your dreams. For instance, if your goal is to travel the world, you can include pictures of your desired destinations, inspiring quotes, and symbols of adventure on your vision board. Each time you glance at it, you reinforce your commitment to achieving your goals.

The brain is capable of being trained, and it can rewire itself. This remarkable capability refers to what is known as **neuroplasticity.** It is the changing of the physical structure, function, and organization of neurons in response to new experiences and memories. These experiences create pathways. Every time we think, feel, or do something, we strengthen this pathway. Habits are well-traveled pathways. New thoughts and skills carve new pathways. Repetition and practice strengthen the pathways by forming new habits. The old pathways get used less and are weakened. With repeated and direct attention towards a desired change, we all have the ability to rewire our brains. Visualization is an efficient and powerful method to reprogram the brain. It is the process of creating a mental image in your mind or rehearsing a planned movement to enhance performance. It helps you achieve your goals by conditioning your brain to see, hear, and feel success. It also reduces performance anxiety, improves your abilities, enhances motivation, and boosts your confidence.

Vision boards can be created using a variety of methods and materials. For example, a physical board placed in an area where you regularly see it or a digital board you place on your devices using different free templates available

How to create and use your vision board

1. Find images that represent your goals. You can go through magazines to find images or look on the internet.

2. Paste the images onto your board. You can arrange them in whatever order you prefer. Avoid using too many words.

3. Embody your goals. Spend at least three minutes twice daily with your board, sensing how it feels to achieve your goals. It's like building muscle; the more you do it, the greater conviction.

4. Imagine and hold that positive emotion longer. The longer you experience those good feelings when you visualize your goal, the less stressed you become, and unbelief is alleviated.

5. Take note of your surroundings. What are the colors? What are the people doing or saying? How is all this making you feel?

6. Repeat your affirmation as you see, hear, and feel yourself accomplishing those goals. Experience the excitement.

Morning Visualization

Starting your day with a visualization exercise can significantly impact your mindset and productivity. Take a few minutes each morning to close your eyes, breathe deeply, and imagine yourself successfully accomplishing your goals. For instance, if your goal is to become a published author, visualize yourself holding a published book, receiving positive reviews, and inspiring readers. Engaging your senses and experiencing the emotions associated with your achievements will strengthen your belief in yourself and set a positive tone for the day.

Setting Daily Intentions

Setting daily intentions is a potent practice that can considerably improve your productivity, concentration, and overall progress toward your larger goals. Rather than letting each day unfold aimlessly, taking a few moments in the morning to set specific intentions can have a profound impact on your business.

You gain clarity on what genuinely matters to you and how your daily actions align with your long-term goals when you begin each day with purpose. By establishing intentions that are directly related to your larger goals, you ensure that each day serves as a stepping stone towards the business you envision.

Practice Affirmations

Affirmations are an empowering technique that can assist in altering one's mindset and shaping one's reality. Affirmations serve as a tool for reprogramming the subconscious mind, replacing limiting beliefs with empowering and positive ones. By incorporating daily affirmations into your routine, you can establish a solid foundation for personal development, increased self-confidence, and a more optimistic outlook on business.

Affirmations serve as reminders of one's inherent value and abilities. By repeatedly affirming your strengths and potential, you develop an intense feeling of self-confidence that permeates many facets of your life. As your self-confidence grows, you become more inclined to accept challenges and pursue new opportunities.

Maintain Consistency and Persistence

Consistency and perseverance are the bedrock upon which visualization and goal-setting can be effectively implemented. These two steadfast characteristics are the forces that propel individuals toward the realization of their plans and aspirations. To realize their maximum potential, it is necessary to transform these practices into daily habits, devoting time and effort to them.

By incorporating visualization into your daily routine, you create a potent mental canvas for creating vivid images of your desired future. Take a few moments each day to immerse yourself in the realm of possibilities, where you see yourself attaining your objectives with absolute clarity. Visualize the specifics of your success while embracing the accompanying emotions: happiness, a sense of accomplishment, and the achievement of your goals. The more frequently you visit this mental sanctuary, the more vibrant the visions become, and the more your subconscious accepts them as attainable realities.

Reflecting and Adjusting

When incorporating visualization and goal-setting into your daily life, reflecting and modifying are crucial pillars of effective implementation. Adopting these practices equips you with a dynamic approach to self-improvement, ensuring that you remain on course and continuously progress toward the achievement of your goals.

Regular reflection is a tool that enables you to take a step back from the daily grind and creates a space for self-awareness and introspection. By devoting time each night to evaluating your progress, you gain valuable insight into the journey. Celebrate your accomplishments and milestones, recognizing the progress you've made toward your objectives. Recognizing your achievements fosters a positive outlook and reinforces your confidence in your ability to succeed.

In summary, incorporating visualization and goal-setting techniques into your daily routine empowers you to create the life you desire. By clarifying your goals, creating vision boards, engaging in morning visualization exercises, setting daily intentions, practicing affirmations, maintaining consistency and persistence, and reflecting on your progress, you will establish a strong foundation for success. Remember, consistent practice and a positive mindset are key to implementing these techniques effectively. So, start today and let visualization and goal-setting become integral parts of your daily routine, guiding you towards a more fulfilling and accomplished life.

LO3: How Staying Focused and Positive Can Propel You to Success

In a world filled with distractions and challenges that can easily derail us from our aspirations, the power of staying focused on our goals and maintaining a positive attitude cannot be underestimated. Clear goals and unwavering commitment to them are essential for achieving success in both personal and professional spheres. Moreover, a positive outlook can serve as a shield against adversity, keeping us motivated and resilient in the face of obstacles that may otherwise derail our progress.

Setting Clear Goals: The Foundation of Success

Setting clear goals is crucial for success in any profession. When we have a clear understanding of what we want to achieve, we can create a well-defined plan to reach our objectives. Setting goals provides direction and purpose, giving us a clear roadmap to success. Without clear goals, we may find ourselves aimlessly wandering, unsure of how to move forward in our careers. Therefore, taking the time to define our goals is the first step towards success.

Maintaining Focus: Overcoming Distractions and Difficulties

Maintaining focus on our goals is equally important. When faced with difficulties, it's easy to become distracted or lose sight of our goals. However, by maintaining focus on our objectives, we can prioritize our efforts and prevent falling prey to the various distractions that come our way. We can stay on track even when faced with unexpected obstacles because we know that every effort we make is bringing us closer to our end goal. Focus helps us allocate our time, energy, and resources effectively, ensuring steady progress towards our aspirations.

The Power of a Positive Outlook: Motivation and Resilience

A positive outlook is also critical for success in any profession. When we maintain a positive mindset, we are better equipped to stay motivated and resilient in the face of challenges. Positivity enables us to approach problems with a can-do attitude, looking for opportunities to learn and grow rather than getting overwhelmed by the difficulties we encounter. By maintaining a positive outlook, we can inspire others around us and create a culture of optimism and positivity in our workplace, which contributes to overall success and well-being.

Marcelo Bielsa's Success Story

One powerful example of the importance of staying focused on goals and maintaining a positive outlook can be found in the story of Marcelo Bielsa, the head coach of the Chilean national soccer team. Bielsa, a legendary figure in South American soccer, was tasked with leading Chile to the World Cup after a 12-year absence from the tournament.

Bielsa faced numerous challenges in achieving this mission. Chile was a relatively small country with a limited talent pool, and the team had a history of underachievement. Additionally, Bielsa had only a limited amount of time to build a cohesive squad and implement his tactics before the World Cup qualifiers began.

Despite these challenges, Bielsa remained focused on his goal and maintained a positive outlook throughout the process. He set clear objectives for his team and worked tirelessly to instill a winning mentality in his players. Bielsa inspired them with his passion, commitment, and attention to detail, creating a culture of excellence within the team.

Bielsa's hard work paid off as Chile qualified for the World Cup in South Africa, and Bielsa was hailed as a hero in his home country. His team played with a style and intensity that captured the imagination of fans around the world, earning widespread praise for their performance.

Bielsa's success is a testament to the power of staying focused on our goals and maintaining a positive outlook, even in the face of daunting challenges. By setting clear objectives and working tirelessly to achieve them, he overcame the obstacles that stood in his way and led his team to success. His unwavering commitment to his goals and his positive attitude served as an inspiration to his players, and his legacy as one of the greatest coaches in South American soccer history remains secure.

In conclusion, staying focused on goals and maintaining a positive outlook are critical for success in any profession. By setting clear objectives and maintaining our focus on them, we create a roadmap to success. Additionally, by maintaining a positive mindset, we can stay motivated and resilient in the face of challenges, creating a culture of optimism and positivity in our workplace. Ultimately, staying focused on goals and maintaining a positive outlook can help us achieve our aspirations and create a fulfilling career. Remember, it's the combination of clear goals, unwavering focus, and a positive attitude that propels us towards success in both our personal and professional lives.

In this chapter, we explored the transformative power of visualization and goal setting in unlocking your wealth mindset. We learned that visualization and goal-setting are powerful tools that can transform your thinking and build sustainable income. By clearly defining your goals and visualizing your desired outcomes, you create a roadmap for success and activate your subconscious mind to work towards achieving those goals.

We explored various techniques for implementing visualization and goal-setting in your daily routine. Creating vision boards, practicing morning visualizations, setting daily intentions, practicing affirmation, and reflecting on your progress are effective ways to integrate these practices into your everyday life. These techniques will help you stay focused, motivated, and aligned with your goals.

We discussed the importance of maintaining focus on your goals and cultivating a positive outlook. With distractions and challenges in the world, staying focused helps you prioritize your efforts and overcome obstacles along the way. A positive mindset enhances your resilience, motivation, and ability to find opportunities in difficult situations.

As we conclude this chapter, let us remember Eleanor Roosevelt's quote: "The future belongs to those who believe in the beauty of their dreams."

Visualization and goal-setting provide the foundation for believing in and achieving your dreams. By incorporating these practices into your daily routine, you can transform your thinking, build sustainable income, and unlock your wealth mindset.

In the next chapter, we will delve deeper into the strategies for overcoming obstacles and maintaining motivation on your journey towards success. Continue reading as we continue to explore the path to realizing your aspirations and creating a fulfilling life.

CHAPTER 4

Winning The Game: Strategies For Sustainable Success

It always seems impossible until it's done.
—**Nelson Mandela**

Learning objectives

This chapter will help you understand the following factors that are critical to unlocking your wealth mindset:

> **LO1:** Learn the importance of conducting thorough market research and be able to apply various methods for gathering and analyzing data.

> **LO2:** Develop a comprehensive strategy that aligns with business goals, incorporating an analysis of strengths, weaknesses, opportunities, and threats.

> **LO3:** Identify potential competitive advantages and develop a plan for leveraging these advantages to differentiate the business from competitors and win in the marketplace.

Success in business doesn't come overnight; it takes strategic planning and execution. In today's fast-paced and highly competitive business world, it is more important than ever for companies to develop a winning strategy that will help them achieve sustainable success. By mastering these key concepts and applying them to your business, you will be able to develop a strategy that aligns with your business goals, differentiates you from your competitors, and positions you for long-term success.

Natura Cosmetics is a Brazilian company that specializes in natural and sustainable beauty products. The company has a strong commitment to sustainability and social responsibility, and this has been a key factor in its success.

To understand its target market, Natura has conducted extensive market research to identify the needs and preferences of its customers. The company has used a variety of research methods, including surveys, focus groups, and in-depth interviews, to gather information about consumer behavior, product preferences, and purchasing habits. Based on this research, Natura has developed a comprehensive marketing strategy that emphasizes the company's commitment to sustainability and social responsibility. This has resonated with consumers, who are increasingly interested in eco-friendly and socially responsible products.

In addition to using market research to guide its marketing strategy, Natura has also used it to inform its product development. The company has launched several successful product lines based on consumer feedback, including its "Ekos" line of natural and sustainable products.

Overall, Natura's commitment to market research has played a key role in its success. By staying in tune with the needs and preferences of its customers, the company has been able to develop products and marketing campaigns that resonate with its audience and drive growth for the business.

LO1: Uncovering Insights through Research

Market research is a critical aspect of any business. It is the process of collecting, analyzing, and interpreting information about a particular market, its consumers, and its competitors. Market research enables businesses to make informed decisions about product development, marketing strategies, pricing, and customer service. Conducting thorough market research is essential to ensuring that businesses are not making uninformed decisions that could lead to their downfall.

Market mastery is essential because it helps businesses understand their target market. Knowing your target market is critical to developing products and services that meet the needs of your customers. Market research enables businesses to identify the demographics of their customers, including their age, gender, income, education level, and location. This information is essential in developing products and services that meet the specific needs of the target market. For example, a business targeting young people will develop products and services that appeal to this age group, such as smartphones, video games, and social media platforms.

The second reason why conducting thorough market research is crucial is that it helps businesses identify potential competitors. Competitor analysis is an essential part of market research, as it helps businesses identify their strengths and weaknesses in comparison to their competitors. Knowing your competitors is critical to developing marketing strategies that differentiate your products and services from those of your competitors. Competitor analysis enables businesses to identify gaps in the market that they can exploit to gain a competitive advantage. For example, a business may identify a gap in the market for affordable and durable smartphones and develop products that will meet this need.

The third reason why conducting thorough market research is crucial is that it helps businesses identify trends in the market. Market trends are changes in the market that can affect the demand for products and services. Knowing market trends is critical to developing products and services that meet the current and future needs of customers. Market research enables businesses to identify trends in the market and develop products and services that meet the changing needs of customers. For example, a business may identify a trend toward sustainable products and develop products that will meet this need.

The fourth reason why conducting thorough market research is essential is that it helps businesses develop effective marketing strategies. Marketing strategies are critical to promoting products and services to customers. Market research enables businesses to identify the most effective marketing channels for reaching their target market. For example, a business targeting young people may identify social media as the most effective marketing channel for reaching this age group. Market research also enables businesses to develop messaging that resonates with their target market, resulting in higher customer engagement and sales.

The fifth reason why conducting thorough market research is essential is that it helps businesses make informed decisions about pricing. Pricing is a critical aspect of marketing strategy, as it affects the demand for products and services. Market research enables businesses to identify the optimal price point for their products and services. For example, a business may conduct a price sensitivity analysis to identify the price points that result in the highest demand for their products and services. Market research also enables businesses to identify pricing strategies that differentiate their products and services from those of their competitors, resulting in higher profitability.

Data Collection and Analysis

There are several methods to gather and analyze data. Below are some of the most common methods.

Surveys: Surveys are questionnaires that are administered to a group of people to gather information about their preferences, behaviors, and opinions. Surveys can be conducted online, through email, or in person.

Interviews: Interviews involve asking individuals or groups of people questions about a specific topic or product to gain insight into their thoughts and opinions. Interviews can be conducted in person, over the phone, or through video conferencing.

Focus groups: Focus groups are a type of qualitative research where a small group of individuals are brought together to discuss a specific topic or product. A facilitator who asks questions and promotes conversation moderates the discussion.

Observational research: This involves observing individuals in their natural environment to gain insights into their behavior and preferences. This can be done in person or through video surveillance.

Data analysis: After gathering data through one or more of the above methods, the data needs to be analyzed to draw conclusions and make decisions. Data analysis can involve statistical analysis, qualitative analysis, or a combination of both.

Overall, the key to successful data gathering and analysis is to use multiple methods to gather diverse data, ensure the data is valid and reliable, and use appropriate analysis techniques to draw insights and make informed decisions.

Case Study: *Revitalizing a Struggling Restaurant*

Background: A local restaurant has been struggling with declining sales and reduced foot traffic. The restaurant owner wants to conduct market research to identify the reasons for the decline and develop strategies to revitalize the business.

Research Objectives: The research objectives for this market research project are as follows:

- ❖ To understand the target audience's preferences and needs regarding dining experiences.
- ❖ To identify the reasons for the decline in sales and reduced foot traffic.
- ❖ To identify new opportunities for growth and expansion.
- ❖ To develop strategies for improving the restaurant's brand image and customer experience.

Target Audience: The target audience for this research project is local residents who dine out frequently and are interested in trying new dining experiences.

Methods for Gathering and Analyzing Data

Surveys: The research team will administer an online survey to gather information about the target audience's dining preferences, needs, and habits. The survey will include questions about their dining preferences, the factors that influence their restaurant choices, and their opinions about the struggling restaurant.

Mystery shopping: The research team will conduct mystery shopping visits to the restaurant to gain insights into the customer experience. The mystery shoppers will evaluate the food quality, service, atmosphere, and cleanliness of the restaurant.

Interviews: The research team will conduct in-depth interviews with regular customers and former customers of the restaurant to identify the reasons for the decline in sales and reduced foot traffic.

Competitor analysis: The research team will analyze the restaurant's competitors to identify new opportunities for growth and expansion.

Data analysis: After gathering data through surveys, mystery shopping, interviews, and competitor analysis, the data will be analyzed using statistical analysis and qualitative analysis. The analysis will identify trends, patterns, and preferences that will inform the restaurant's development and marketing strategies.

Recommendations:

❖ Update the restaurant's menu to include more vegetarian and vegan options to cater to the changing dining preferences of customers.

❖ Enhance the restaurant's customer experience by improving the service, atmosphere, and cleanliness.

❖ Develop a loyalty program to reward regular customers and encourage repeat visits.

❖ Expand the restaurant's marketing efforts to target a wider audience through social media and local advertising.

❖ Leverage the restaurant's location by partnering with local events and organizations to increase brand awareness and drive foot traffic.

Conclusion:

Thorough market research is critical to identifying the reasons for declining sales and reduced foot traffic at a struggling restaurant. By conducting surveys, mystery shopping, interviews, and competitor analysis, the research team can gain valuable insights into the target audience's preferences and needs. The data analysis will identify trends and patterns that will inform the restaurant's development and marketing strategies. By implementing the recommendations based on the findings, the restaurant can revitalize its business, improve its brand image, and provide a better dining experience to its customers.

Case Study: *Launching a New Fitness App*

Background: A startup company wants to launch a new fitness app that provides personalized workout plans and nutrition advice based on individual needs and goals. The company needs to conduct market research to determine the potential demand for the app, understand the target audience's preferences, and identify the best marketing channels to reach the target audience.

Research Objectives: The research objectives for this market research project are as follows:

- ❖ To determine the potential demand for the fitness app in the target market.

- ❖ To understand the target audience's preferences and needs regarding fitness apps.

- ❖ To identify the most effective marketing channels to reach the target audience.

- ❖ To determine the price point that would be acceptable to the target audience.

- ❖ Target Audience: The target audience for this research project is adults between the ages of 18 and 40 who are interested in fitness and use mobile apps.

Methods for Gathering and Analyzing Data

Surveys: The research team will administer an online survey to gather information about the target audience's preferences, needs, and habits regarding fitness apps. The survey will include questions about their current fitness routines, their preferred types of workouts, and their preferred features in a fitness app. The survey will also ask about their willingness to pay for a fitness app and their preferred marketing channels.

Focus groups: The research team will conduct focus groups to gain deeper insights into the target audience's preferences and needs. The focus groups will consist of 8–10 participants and will be held in person or online. A facilitator will moderate the focus groups and elicit feedback on the proposed app's features as well as the target audience's experiences with fitness apps.

Data analysis: After gathering data through surveys and focus groups, the data will be analyzed using statistical analysis and qualitative analysis. The analysis will identify trends, patterns, and preferences that will inform the app's development and marketing strategies.

Recommendations:

- ❖ Develop an app that provides personalized workout plans and nutrition advice based on individual needs and goals.
- ❖ Price the app at $9.99 per month, as this is the price point that is most acceptable to the target audience.
- ❖ Advertise the app through social media, as this is the preferred marketing channel for the target audience.
- ❖ Include features such as progress tracking, community support, and rewards to attract and retain users.
- ❖ Launch a free trial period to encourage people to try the app and provide feedback for further improvement.

Conclusion:

Thorough market research is crucial for the success of any product launch, including a fitness app. By conducting surveys and focus groups, the research team can gain valuable insights into the target audience's preferences and needs. The data analysis will identify trends and patterns that will inform the app's development and marketing strategies. By implementing the recommendations based on the findings, the startup company can launch a successful fitness app that meets the target audience's needs and preferences.

LO2: Crafting a Comprehensive Business Strategy that Works

Crafting a comprehensive strategy that works requires a thorough analysis of the company's internal and external environment. This can be done by conducting a SWOT analysis that evaluates the company's strengths, weaknesses, opportunities, and threats. The following is a step-by-step guide for creating a comprehensive strategy that aligns with business goals.

Step 1: Identify Business Goals

The first step is to identify the company's business goals. This involves understanding the company's mission, vision, and objectives. Business goals should be specific, measurable, achievable, relevant, and time-bound (SMART).

Step 2: Conduct a SWOT Analysis

A SWOT analysis is a useful tool for assessing the company's internal and external environment. This analysis should identify the company's **s**trengths, **w**eaknesses, **o**pportunities, and **t**hreats.

Strengths: These are the company's internal resources and capabilities that give it a competitive advantage. This could include a strong brand, efficient processes, a skilled workforce, and innovative products or services.

Weaknesses: These are the internal factors that hinder the company's ability to achieve its goals. This could include outdated technology, limited resources, poor management, or a lack of innovation.

Opportunities: These are external factors that the company can capitalize on to achieve its goals. This could include new markets, emerging trends, or changing customer needs.

Threats: These are external factors that pose a risk to the company's success. This could include competitors, economic downturns, or changing regulations.

Set aside about an hour and conduct a SWOT analysis for your company. The table below provides questions for you to consider in each section.

Strengths	Weaknesses
• What advantages does the business have over others? • What is likely to produce the greatest return on investment? • What does the business do well? • What would be the best thing to implement quickly? • If we are not looking at an obvious area, why not?	• What are the areas where we should and could do better? • Which areas should we avoid altogether? • What do our customers consistently complain about? • What do our employees consistently complain about? • Do we have any internal or external processes that are obviously slow?

Opportunities	Threats
• What are the obvious opportunities we can see? • What are the current exciting trends in the marketplace? • What are the predicted long-term trends in the market and technology? • Are there any social, lifestyle, or population changes we can exploit? • What is happening with our existing development programs?	• What are the biggest external obstacles we face? • What are our competitors doing? • Are there any government/regulatory changes we need to note? • Can we keep up with technological changes? • How good is our relationship with our suppliers?

Step 3: Develop a Strategy

Based on the SWOT analysis, develop a strategy that aligns with the company's goals. The strategy should leverage the company's strengths, address its weaknesses, capitalize on opportunities, and mitigate threats. This could involve one or more of the following strategies:

Growth strategy: This involves expanding the company's products or services, entering new markets, or acquiring other companies.

Cost leadership strategy: This involves reducing costs to offer products or services at a lower price than competitors.

Differentiation strategy: This involves offering unique products or services that stand out from competitors.

Innovation strategy: This involves investing in research and development to create new products or services or improve existing ones.

Collaboration strategy: This involves partnering with other companies or organizations to achieve common goals.

Step 4: Implementing the Strategy

Once the strategy is developed, it is important to implement it effectively. This involves setting specific goals, assigning responsibilities, allocating resources, and monitoring progress. The implementation of the strategy should be flexible enough to adapt to changing circumstances.

Step 5: Evaluation of the Strategy

Finally, it is important to evaluate the effectiveness of the strategy regularly. This involves measuring progress against goals, identifying areas for improvement, and making necessary adjustments to the strategy. This ongoing evaluation ensures that the company's strategy remains aligned with its goals and is effective in achieving them.

Natura & Co. has a strong commitment to sustainability and social responsibility, which are key parts of its business strategy. The company regularly evaluates its strategies and initiatives to ensure that they are aligned with its values and goals. In recent years, Natura & Co. has made several strategic acquisitions, including The Body Shop and Avon, which have helped the company expand its global reach and increase its market share. The company has also invested in digital technology to improve its customer experience and streamline its operations.

These strategic moves have paid off for Natura & Co., with the company reporting strong financial performance and growth in recent years. In 2020, the company's net revenue increased by 12.2% compared to the previous year, despite the challenges posed by the COVID-19 pandemic.

Overall, Natura & Co.'s commitment to sustainability, social responsibility, and strategic evaluation has helped it succeed in a competitive market and has positioned itself for continued growth in the future.

LO3: The Road to Market Domination

It is not enough to simply offer a good product or service in today's fiercely competitive marketplace. To truly stand out and succeed, businesses must identify and capitalize on their unique strengths and advantages over their competitors. This makes the concept of competitive advantage essential to dominating the marketplace. Competitive advantage refers to the factors that set a business apart from its competitors and make it more appealing to customers. These factors could be anything from product features, pricing strategy, customer service, distribution channels, brand reputation, or any other aspect that provides added value to customers.

Leveraging their competitive advantage, businesses can differentiate themselves from competitors and dominate their market. This requires a comprehensive understanding of the market landscape, customer needs, and the strengths and weaknesses of the competition.

It is essential for long-term success to develop a strategic plan that leverages a business's unique strengths to create a sustainable competitive advantage. This involves aligning the business's goals, resources, and capabilities with customer needs and market opportunities. With a well-executed plan, businesses can effectively differentiate themselves, increase market share, and drive growth.

How To Identify Potential Competitive Advantages

It is important to conduct a thorough analysis of the business, its products or services, and the market in which it operates. Some possible areas to consider include:

Unique Product or Service Offering: Does the business offer a product or service that is different from what is currently available on the market? If so, this could be a significant competitive advantage.

Brand Recognition: Does the business have a strong brand that is well-known and trusted by customers? A strong brand can differentiate a business from its competitors and help it win market share.

Cost Advantage: Does the business have a cost advantage over its competitors? For example, is it able to produce its products or services at a lower cost due to economies of scale, proprietary technology, or other factors?

Customer Experience: Does the business provide a superior customer experience compared to its competitors? This could include factors such as ease of use, personalized service, or exceptional customer support.

Innovation: Is the business at the forefront of innovation in its industry? If so, this could give it a significant competitive advantage by allowing it to offer products or services that are more advanced or unique than those available from competitors.

Develop a Plan

Once potential competitive advantages have been identified, the next step is to develop a plan for leveraging these advantages to differentiate the business from competitors and win in the marketplace. Some possible strategies to consider include:

Focus on Marketing: If the business has a unique product or service offering or a strong brand, it may be able to leverage this through targeted marketing campaigns that highlight these strengths.

Streamline Operations: If the business has a cost advantage, it may be able to further reduce costs and increase efficiency by streamlining operations or implementing new technology.

Invest in Customer Service: If the business provides a superior customer experience, it may be able to further differentiate itself by investing in customer service training or tools that allow for more personalized service.

Continue Innovating: If the business is at the forefront of innovation in its industry, it should continue to invest in research and development to stay ahead of competitors and maintain its competitive advantage.

Expand Product or Service Offerings: If the business has a unique product or service offering, it may be able to expand this offering to attract new customers and increase market share.

In summary, the key to leveraging competitive advantages is to continually assess the market and the competition and adjust strategies as necessary to maintain a competitive edge.

In this chapter, we identify the essential strategies for achieving sustainable success and unlocking your wealth mindset. We emphasized the significance of conducting thorough market research as a foundation for success. By gathering and analyzing relevant data, you gain valuable insights into market trends, customer needs, and competitor analysis. This knowledge allows you to make informed decisions and adapt your strategies to meet market demands.

We explored the process of developing a comprehensive strategy that aligns with your business goals. This involves conducting a SWOT analysis (**S**trengths, **W**eaknesses, **O**pportunities, and **T**hreats) to assess your internal capabilities and external environment. By understanding your strengths and weaknesses, you can capitalize on opportunities and mitigate potential threats, setting a clear path for sustainable success.

We discussed the importance of identifying and leveraging competitive advantages to differentiate your business from competitors. Whether it's unique products or services, superior customer service, cost leadership, or technological innovations, recognizing your competitive advantages will allow you to carve a niche in the market and attract customers. Developing a plan to leverage these advantages will strengthen your position and enhance your chances of winning in the marketplace.

As we conclude this chapter, let us remember Nelson Mandela's quote: "It always seems impossible until it's done." The strategies outlined in this chapter provide you with the tools and insights to overcome challenges and achieve sustainable success. By conducting thorough market research, developing a comprehensive strategy, and leveraging competitive advantages, you can navigate the marketplace with confidence and achieve your wealth mindset goals.

In the next chapter, we will explore the crucial aspects of navigating uncertainty to ensure long-term success. Well done on reaching so far as we continue our journey towards sustainable and prosperous endeavors.

Activity:
Strategies to identify what makes you unique

Define your target audience: Before you can identify what makes your business unique, you need to define who your target audience is. Think about who your ideal customers are and identify their needs and wants.

Brainstorm your unique selling proposition (USP): Ask yourself what sets your business apart from others in your industry. Is it your product or service, your customer service, your pricing, or something else? Write down all the ideas that come to mind.

Conduct a SWOT analysis: A SWOT analysis is a tool that can help you identify your business's strengths, weaknesses, opportunities, and threats. This analysis will help you identify your unique features as well as areas where you can improve.

Conduct market research: find out what your customers think of your business, your competitors, and your industry. This will help you identify what your customers value about your business and what sets you apart from the competition.

Create a brand personality: Your brand personality is the unique voice, tone, and style that sets your business apart from others. Define your brand's personality traits, such as being friendly, innovative, or trustworthy, and make sure they are reflected in all of your marketing materials.

Create a positioning statement: A positioning statement is a concise statement that describes your business's unique value proposition and why your target audience should choose your business over others in your industry. It should be easy to remember and communicate.

Review and refine: Once you've completed the previous steps, review your findings and refine your USP, brand personality, and positioning statement as needed. Use this information to guide your marketing and branding efforts to stand out in your industry.

CHAPTER 5

Navigating Uncertainty

Persistence breaks resistance and paves the path to success.
—Tannizia Gasper

Learning Objectives

This chapter will help you understand the following factors that are critical to unlocking your wealth mindset:

LO1: Learn to build resilience to change and adaptability to unpredictable circumstances.

LO2: Institute strategies for managing ambiguity and uncertainty in decision-making processes.

LO3: Develop a growth mindset and embrace experimentation and innovation as a means to navigate uncertainty, rather than fearing failure or avoiding risks.

The world is changing faster than ever before, and uncertainty is the new normal. From global pandemics to rapid technological advances, the pace of change can be overwhelming, leaving individuals and organizations struggling to keep up. But what if uncertainty could be harnessed as a source of opportunity and growth, rather than a threat?

In this chapter, we'll explore three key learning objectives for navigating uncertainty: *building resilience, managing ambiguity, and embracing experimentation and innovation.* These objectives will provide readers with the tools and mindset needed to not only survive, but thrive in uncertain environments.

LO1: Building Resilience in the Face of Change

The ability to adapt to change and unpredictable circumstances is becoming increasingly critical for individuals and organizations in today's fast-paced world. With technological advancements, globalization, and other external factors, change has become a constant and unpredictable phenomenon. Therefore, it is crucial to build resilience to change and develop adaptability skills to navigate through these challenging times.

Resilience is the ability to bounce back from difficult situations, adapt to new circumstances, and emerge stronger than before. Building resilience is critical for individuals and organizations to survive and thrive in challenging situations. Adversity can come in many forms, such as financial hardship, unexpected losses, natural disasters, or global pandemics. Developing resilience skills can help individuals and organizations cope with such situations.

Adaptability, on the other hand, refers to the ability to adjust and change one's behavior, thinking, or approach to fit changing circumstances. It involves being open to new ideas, being flexible, and being able to learn quickly. The ability to adapt is essential for individuals and organizations to remain competitive in today's dynamic and ever-changing environment.

In order to build resilience and adaptability, individuals and organizations can take several steps. Firstly, it is essential to build a strong support network. Surround yourself with a strong network of mentors, advisors, and peers who can offer guidance and support when times get tough. It can also provide organizations with access to resources and expertise that they may not have on their own.

Secondly, prioritize self-care. Running a business can be stressful, so it's important to prioritize your own self-care. Make time for exercise, mindfulness, and other stress-reducing activities to help you stay focused and resilient.

Thirdly, foster a positive company culture. A positive company culture can help build resistance by creating a sense of community and support among your team members. This can help everyone stay motivated and focused during difficult times.

Fourthly, develop a contingency plan. Contingency plans involve anticipating potential problems or challenges and developing a plan of action to address them. It can help individuals and organizations be better prepared for unexpected situations and reduce the impact of potential disruptions.

Finally, individuals and organizations can embrace change and take calculated risks. Change is inevitable, and individuals and organizations that embrace change are more likely to adapt and thrive in changing circumstances. Taking calculated risks can also help individuals and organizations innovate and find new opportunities for growth and development.

In conclusion, building resilience to change and developing adaptability skills are critical for individuals and organizations to survive and thrive in today's dynamic environment. To build resilience and adaptability, individuals and organizations can develop a growth mindset, practice mindfulness, build a strong support network, develop contingency plans, embrace change, and take calculated risks. By implementing these strategies, individuals and organizations can develop the skills they need to navigate through challenging times and emerge stronger than before.

Turning Challenges into Opportunities

Dennis Mohammed and his family faced a major challenge when they experienced a job loss while living in a foreign country. Mr. Mohammed was employed in a foreign country while his wife lost her job as a pharmacist as she was pursuing her dream of becoming a medical doctor. With three young children to support, they knew they had to act fast. Together, they decided to start a pharmacy business, with Mrs. Mohammed as the resident pharmacist.

Despite the fact that he had no experience in the pharmacy industry, they were determined to make their dream a reality. They pitched their idea to a friend who believed in them and lent them the capital to start their business. With a small amount of stock and a 10x12 space, they began their journey.

However, their journey was not without challenges. They struggled to pay their bills on time, had difficulty ordering a variety of stock, and couldn't always pay themselves. But they never lost sight of their philosophy of service over money. They were always charitable and put their customers first, and that is what helped them retain their loyal customer base.

Their exceptional service set them apart from the competition, and they soon gained a reputation for going above and beyond for their customers.

They greeted every customer on arrival, said thank you after a sale, and even helped those who couldn't afford their services. They believed that adapting these small but powerful principles would make all the difference.

The family's hard work and dedication paid off, and they soon grew their business beyond their wildest dreams. Mr. Mohammed even returned to school to pursue a certification in phlebotomy, which helped reduce their operating costs by not having to outsource the skill.

Looking back, the family realized that their setback was actually a blessing in disguise. They embraced the challenges and learned from them. That has helped them become successful entrepreneurs. Today, they are proud of the growth and learning opportunities they embraced along the way. Their story is a testament to the power of determination, hard work, and perseverance. Dennis Mohammed is a strong believer that a moral life leads to success.

LO2: Mastering Decision-Making in Uncertain Times

Managing ambiguity and uncertainty is an essential skill in decision-making processes, especially in complex and rapidly changing environments. Here are some strategies for managing ambiguity and uncertainty in decision-making processes:

Gather relevant information: When faced with ambiguity and uncertainty, it's essential to gather as much relevant information as possible. This includes both qualitative and quantitative data from a variety of sources, such as market trends, customer feedback, and expert opinions. Gathering diverse perspectives can help identify blind spots and potential biases.

Identify patterns and trends: Analyzing the information gathered can help identify patterns and trends that can inform decision-making. It's essential to remain open-minded and consider alternative interpretations and explanations for the data.

Consider multiple options: When facing ambiguity and uncertainty, it's crucial to consider multiple options and scenarios. This can help to anticipate potential outcomes and prepare for different eventualities.

Use scenario planning. Scenario planning involves creating multiple plausible scenarios that can occur in the future. This can help identify potential risks and opportunities and prepare for different outcomes.

Focus on what's within your control. When faced with ambiguity and uncertainty, it's important to focus on what you can control. This includes identifying areas where you have influence and taking action to mitigate risks.

Involve others: Involving others in the decision-making process can help reduce ambiguity and uncertainty. This includes seeking input from experts, stakeholders, and team members. Encouraging diverse perspectives and open communication can help identify blind spots and enhance the quality of decision-making.

Remain agile: In rapidly changing environments, it's essential to remain agile and adaptable. This means being willing to adjust plans and strategies as new information emerges, being open to feedback, and learning from mistakes.

By employing these strategies, individuals and organizations can better manage ambiguity and uncertainty in decision-making processes and make more informed and effective decisions.

LO3: Overcoming Fear of Failure

Uncertainty is a constant companion in our fast-paced world of business. Entrepreneurs and business owners face a wide array of challenges on a daily basis, from market fluctuations to changing consumer demands. Navigating these uncertainties requires a mindset that is adaptable, innovative, and growth-oriented. Rather than fearing failure or avoiding risks, successful business owners embrace experimentation and innovation as a means to navigate uncertainty. We will explore the concept of a growth mindset and the ways in which it can help business owners overcome the challenges of uncertainty.

A growth mindset is a way of thinking that emphasizes the potential for growth and learning, even in the face of setbacks and challenges. It is characterized by a willingness to take on new challenges, a belief in the power of effort and perseverance, and a focus on continuous improvement. In contrast, a fixed mindset is a way of thinking that assumes that abilities and qualities are fixed and unchangeable. This type of mindset can lead to a fear of failure and a reluctance to take risks.

Business owners adopting a growth mindset is essential for success in today's uncertain business environment. By embracing experimentation and innovation, business owners can stay ahead of the curve and capitalize on emerging opportunities. They can also navigate challenges and setbacks more effectively, using them as opportunities for growth and learning.

The mindset of a successful entrepreneur

Entrepreneurs who are successful know that their thoughts shape their reality. They understand that we become what we think about and actively work to cultivate a growth mindset. By adopting this principle, they are able to navigate uncertainty with ease, embrace experimentation and innovation, and ultimately achieve their goals. Some characteristics of a successful entrepreneur are:

Resilience

Resiliency develops as you embrace change after failure in your business. You must know, **it is not failure that will break you, it's your response.** Recognizing that failure is common to the human journey, it must be used as a setup for your comeback. It creates proficiency in your creativity and innovation and gives you the determination to keep going despite obstacles.

Risk takers and visionary

One of the key benefits of a growth mindset is that it encourages a willingness to take risks. Entrepreneurs are a unique breed of individuals who possess a strong drive to succeed. They have a clear vision of what they want to achieve and work tirelessly to make it a reality. When they are open to experimentation and innovation, they are more likely to take calculated risks in pursuit of new opportunities. This willingness to take risks can lead to breakthroughs and innovations that would not have been possible with a fixed mindset.

Develop creativity and innovation

Entrepreneurs with a growth mindset are more likely to embrace experimentation and try new approaches to problem-solving. This can lead to more creative and effective solutions to challenges that arise in the business environment. It develops a *'no matter what'* attitude.

Foster a Culture of Learning and Continuous improvement

When entrepreneurs view setbacks and challenges as opportunities for growth and learning, they are more likely to invest in their own education and development as well as that of their employees. This can lead to a more skilled and adaptable workforce as well as a more dynamic and innovative business culture.

Display passion and self-motivation

The satisfaction of producing something original and significant also serves as a driving force for them. **Passion and commitment to their ideas are frequently what motivate entrepreneurs.** They have a burning desire to bring their vision to life and are willing to put in the necessary effort to make it happen. This drive is often what sets them apart from others in their field. Furthermore, entrepreneurs are self-motivated individuals who do not rely on external factors to drive their work. The satisfaction of producing something original and significant also serves as a driving force for them. This intrinsic motivation helps them push through obstacles and setbacks and maintain focus on their goals.

Update with industry trends

Stay informed about the latest developments in your industry and look for opportunities to innovate and capitalize on new technologies. Review consumer spending and economic indicators to identify market trends and scope. Research your industry and target market to identify trends and gaps in the market that your business can fill.

Monitor market conditions

It is important to be knowledgeable about what your competitors are doing and look for ways to differentiate your business and offer something unique. Study your competitors' strengths and weaknesses and identify areas where you can offer a better solution.

Pay attention to customer feedback

Feedback can identify areas where the business is not performing and provide an opportunity for improvement. It causes the business to turn a weakness into a strength or even an opportunity by creating a new product or service. Acting on feedback shows that the business values its customers and is committed to their satisfaction. This creates trust and increases their loyalty. Feedback provides insight into what motivates customers to buy and what turns them off, which can then inform marketing strategies.

Embrace failure as a natural part of the growth process

Successful entrepreneurs understand that failure is not the opposite of success but rather a crucial part of the journey towards it. To achieve success, entrepreneurs must shift their perspective on failure and view it as an opportunity for growth and learning. They must adopt a growth mindset that allows them to embrace failure as a means of improving themselves and their businesses. To help entrepreneurs reframe their perspective on failure, below is a *new* meaning of failure that can serve as a guide.

F- Face your challenges head on.

A- Assess the current situation and your future expectations.

I- Intentional actions towards your goals

L-Learn from your mistakes.

U- Understand your unique value and rebuild.

R- Reinvent yourself to do the work!

E- Embrace an example to emulate.

The first step in this guide is to face challenges head-on. Rather than avoiding or ignoring challenges, entrepreneurs must confront them head-on and be willing to take risks in pursuit of their goals.

The second step is to assess the current situation and future expectations. Particularly, entrepreneurs recognize the significance of conducting a comprehensive evaluation of their current standing. By analyzing their strengths, weaknesses, opportunities, and threats objectively, they obtain valuable insights into their market position and growth potential.

Entrepreneurs identify any voids in their knowledge, skills, or resources that may be impeding their progress through this evaluation. By recognizing these areas for development, they set the groundwork for deliberate actions toward their objectives. This self-awareness fosters a proactive attitude, enabling them to devise effective strategies to reconcile the gaps.

The third step is to take intentional actions towards their goals. This requires a willingness to take risks and try new things, even if they may result in failure. Entrepreneurs must have the courage to step outside of their comfort zone and take action towards their goals.

The fourth step is to learn from mistakes. When entrepreneurs experience setbacks or failures, they must analyze what went wrong and learn from those mistakes. This learning allows them to make better decisions and take smarter risks in the future.

The fifth step is to understand their unique value and rebuild. Entrepreneurs must identify their unique strengths and talents and leverage them to create value for their customers. When faced with failure, they can use this knowledge to rebuild and improve their businesses.

The sixth step is to reinvent themselves and do the work. Entrepreneurship is a constantly evolving process, and successful entrepreneurs must be willing to reinvent themselves and their businesses to stay ahead of the curve. This requires hard work, dedication, and a willingness to embrace change.

The seventh and final step is to embrace an example to emulate. Entrepreneurs must seek out role models and mentors who have achieved success in their fields. By learning from those who have gone before them, entrepreneurs can gain valuable insights and guidance that can help them on their own journey towards success.

In conclusion, successful entrepreneurs understand that failure is not the end but rather a stepping stone towards success. By adopting a growth mindset and shifting their perspective on failure, entrepreneurs can learn from their mistakes, take risks, and ultimately achieve their goals. The attached new meaning of failure serves as a guide for entrepreneurs to face challenges head-on: assess their situation, take intentional actions, learn from their mistakes, understand their unique value, reinvent themselves, and seek out role models to emulate.

In this chapter, we explored the essential skills and mindset needed to navigate uncertainty successfully and unlock your wealth mindset. We emphasized the importance of building resilience to change and developing adaptability in unpredictable circumstances. The ability to bounce back from setbacks, embrace change, and adjust your strategies is crucial to navigating uncertain times. By cultivating resilience and adaptability, you can face challenges with confidence and find new opportunities for growth.

We discussed strategies for managing ambiguity and uncertainty in decision-making processes. Uncertainty is an inherent part of life and business, and it is essential to approach it with a clear and rational mindset. By gathering information, considering multiple perspectives, and using tools like scenario planning, you can make informed decisions even in uncertain situations.

We explored the concept of a growth mindset and its significance in navigating uncertainty. Embracing a growth mindset means viewing challenges as opportunities for learning and growth rather than fearing failure or avoiding risks. By embracing experimentation and innovation, you can adapt to changing circumstances, discover new solutions, and seize opportunities that arise in uncertain times.

Remember Tannizia Gasper's quote: "Persistence breaks resistance and paves the path to success." Navigating uncertainty requires persistence, resilience, and a willingness to adapt. By building resilience, managing ambiguity, and embracing a growth mindset, you can navigate uncertain situations with confidence and unlock your wealth mindset.

In the next chapter, we will explore the importance of financial management and strategies for overcoming financial challenges to achieve sustainable success. Let's continue on the journey towards realizing your aspirations and creating a thriving future.

CHAPTER 6

Building a Strong Financial Future

There is no passion to be found in playing small—in settling for a life that is less than the one you are capable of living. **—Nelson Mandela**

Learning Objectives

This chapter will help you understand the following factors that are critical to unlocking your wealth mindset:

LO1: Learn the importance of financial planning in building lasting wealth and the potential consequences of not having a plan.

LO2: Identify strategies to overcome common financial obstacles and challenges.

LO3: Identifying opportunities to increase income and build wealth

Overcoming Financial Hurdles and Ensuring Sustainability

Guyana's sugar industry, GuySuCo is a vital source of employment and income for rural communities, but has been facing severe financial challenges due to declining production and revenues. The declining global demand for sugar, coupled with rising production costs and the need for modernization, has made it particularly difficult for GuySuCo to keep up.

To address these challenges, the government announced a restructuring plan in 2017, which included shutting down several sugar estates and reducing the workforce. However, this plan has faced opposition from workers and trade unions, who argue that it will result in job losses and economic hardship for affected communities.

In response to its financial difficulties, GuySuCo has implemented measures to diversify into other crops and modernize its operations, adopting new technologies and management practices to improve efficiency and reduce costs. However, these measures have not been enough to overcome the challenges facing the industry, and the company reported a loss of over $12 billion in Guyanese dollars in 2019.

The struggles of GuySuCo have significant implications for the country's economy, particularly for rural communities that rely on the industry for employment and income. The government and industry stakeholders are working to find solutions to ensure the long-term sustainability of the industry, including the development of new markets and the promotion of value-added products. Opportunities for innovation and growth exist, which could help secure the industry's future.

LO1: Future Proof Finances

Financial planning is a critical aspect of building lasting wealth and achieving financial security. It involves creating a strategy for managing your finances, setting financial goals, and developing a roadmap for achieving those goals. While financial planning may seem daunting, the potential consequences of not having a plan can be even more significant.

One of the key benefits of **financial planning is that it provides a framework for making informed financial decisions.** With a financial plan in place, you can set specific goals, such as paying off debt or buying a home, and develop a strategy for achieving those goals. This approach can help you avoid impulsive or poorly thought-out financial decisions that could have long-term consequences. It helps in setting realistic goals in areas including projected revenue, profit margins, and cash flow targets. This allows them to plan and allocate resources effectively to achieve these goals.

Financial planning provides clarity on business finances. It gives small business owners a clear understanding of the state of their finances, which include income, expenses, profits, and cash flow. This knowledge enables them to make informed decisions regarding resource allocation, investments, and managing debt.

In addition, **financial planning can help you manage financial risks and protect your assets.** By identifying potential risks, such as market volatility or unexpected expenses, you can develop strategies for mitigating those risks, such as diversifying your investments or creating an emergency fund. This can help you avoid financial setbacks that could jeopardize your long-term financial security.

Another benefit of financial planning is that it can help you build wealth over time. By setting financial goals and developing a plan for achieving those goals, you can take concrete steps towards building wealth, such as investing in stocks or real estate or growing your business. Over time, these investments can compound and grow, providing a solid foundation for lasting financial security. By managing cash flow through forecasting and regular monitoring, businesses can take proactive steps to ensure that they have enough cash on hand to meet their financial obligations.

Financial planning facilitates growth and expansion. Small businesses need to grow and expand to remain competitive and profitable. It provides a roadmap for achieving growth and expansion goals by identifying the necessary resources, funding requirements, and financial metrics for measuring success. A robust financial plan demonstrates that a business has a clear understanding of its financial position, objectives, and plans for achieving success. This, in turn, makes the business a more attractive investment opportunity.

In summary, financial planning is critical to the success of small businesses. It provides a clear understanding of business finances, helps manage cash flow, facilitates efficient resource allocation, enables growth and expansion, and attracts investment.

Budget Creation and Cash Flow Management

Entrepreneurs face unique financial challenges when it comes to managing their cash flow. As a business owner, it's essential to not only create a personal budget but also a separate budget for your business. The following are some steps that entrepreneurs can take to create a budget and manage their cash flow effectively:

The first step in creating a budget as an entrepreneur is to determine your personal monthly income. This includes your salary or wages from your business as well as any other sources of personal income. Once you have determined your personal income, you can start to look at your personal expenses. In my experience, many business owners don't pay themselves for the work they do; instead, the business supports their way of life. This is a major pitfall that can cause a business to struggle to maintain a sustainable income.

The second step is to track your personal expenses for a few months to get a clear understanding of where your money is going. This includes fixed expenses such as rent or mortgage payments, utilities, and insurance, as well as variable expenses such as groceries, dining out, and entertainment. For example, if you find that you are spending a significant amount of money on dining out, you could consider cutting back and cooking more meals at home.

The third step is to create a personal budget based on your income and expenses. Start by subtracting your personal expenses from your personal income to determine your personal net cash flow. Then, allocate your net cash flow to different personal expense categories, such as housing, transportation, food, and entertainment. Make sure to include a category for personal savings and emergency expenses. For example, if your personal net cash flow is $3,000 per month, you might allocate $1,200 for housing, $500 for transportation, $400 for food, $200 for entertainment, and $700 for personal savings and emergency expenses.

The fourth step is to create a separate budget for your business. Start by determining your monthly business income and expenses. This includes revenue from sales, investments, and any other sources, as well as expenses such as salaries, rent, utilities, and inventory costs. Allocate your business's net cash flow to different business expense categories, such as marketing, research and development, and equipment purchases. Make sure to include a category for business savings and emergency expenses. For example, if your business's net cash flow is $10,000 per month, you might allocate $4,000 for salaries, $2,000 for rent and utilities, $2,000 for marketing, $1,000 for research and development, $500 for equipment purchases, and $500 for business savings and emergency expenses.

Once you have created your personal and business budgets, it is important to stick to them. This means tracking your expenses on a regular basis to ensure that you are staying within your budget. If you find that you are overspending in a particular category, look for ways to cut back. For example, if you find that you are spending too much money on transportation, you could consider carpooling, taking public transportation, or downsizing to a more affordable vehicle.

Cash Flow Management

Cash flow is a critical factor for the success of any business, and it is often said that "cash is king." Without cash, a business cannot survive, as it is the lifeblood that keeps it running. Generating enough cash from business activities is crucial to meet expenses, repay investors, and fund growth. Unlike earnings, which can be manipulated, cash flow provides an accurate picture of a business's financial health. Therefore, managing cash flow effectively is essential for entrepreneurs to sustain and grow their businesses. There are several steps that entrepreneurs can take to manage their cash flow effectively.

It is vital to **build an emergency fund for both personal and business expenses**. This fund should have enough money to cover three to six months' worth of living expenses and business expenses in the event of a job loss, illness, or other unexpected expense.

Another important step is to **monitor your cash flow on a regular basis**. Keep track of your accounts receivable and payable to ensure that you are getting paid on time and paying your bills on time. Delayed payments can cause serious cash flow problems for your business. It's also essential to have a cash reserve for your business that you can tap into in case of emergencies or unexpected expenses.

It is important to **be proactive about managing your cash flow** as an entrepreneur. This means regularly reviewing your budgets, tracking your expenses, and making adjustments as needed. It also means being mindful of your spending and making informed financial decisions based on your budget and financial goals.

In brief, **managing your cash flow effectively is essential to achieving financial stability and long-term success.** By tracking your income and expenses, creating a budget, and sticking to it, you can gain control over your finances and make informed financial decisions. With discipline, planning, and a little bit of effort, anyone can create a budget and manage their cash flow effectively.

The Cost of Financial Neglect

Financial neglect can have significant repercussions. Without a plan, you may struggle to make informed financial decisions or prioritize your financial goals. This can lead to missed opportunities to invest in your business, such as hiring new employees, launching new products or services, or expanding into new markets. It can limit your business's growth potential and competitive edge.

If you don't have a financial plan, it can be harder to secure funding from investors or lenders, as they may see your business as risky or poorly managed. This can limit your ability to grow and expand your business. In addition, you may overlook important legal and tax obligations, such as filing tax returns on time or complying with employment regulations. This can result in fines, legal fees, and damage to your business's reputation.

In addition, without a plan in place, you may be more vulnerable to financial risks, unexpected expenses, and business failure. It can be difficult to manage your cash flow, make strategic decisions, and plan for future expenses. This can put your business at risk of failure, especially during difficult economic times or unexpected events. For example, if you don't have an emergency fund, an unexpected medical expense or car repair could leave you in a difficult financial situation. Similarly, if you don't have a diversified investment portfolio, market volatility could significantly impact your investments.

As an entrepreneur, your personal finances are often closely tied to your business finances. Without a financial plan, you may struggle to manage your personal finances, including paying off debt, saving for scaling your business, or covering unexpected expenses.

Overall, the importance of financial planning for building lasting wealth cannot be overstated. A well-crafted financial plan can help you make informed financial decisions, manage risks, and build wealth over time. In contrast, not having a plan can lead to missed opportunities, financial setbacks, and a lack of financial security. By taking the time to develop a financial plan, you can set yourself on a path towards lasting financial stability and prosperity.

Case Study: How Financial Planning Can Aid a Struggling Business in Building Lasting Wealth

ABC Construction Company is a small business that provides construction services to clients in the local area. The business has been struggling to grow and generate profits due to fierce competition, rising material costs, and difficulties in securing financing.

The owners of ABC Construction Company realize that they need to take a more proactive approach to managing their finances if they want to turn their business around and build lasting wealth. They decide to seek professional financial advice.

After consulting with a financial planner, the owners of ABC Construction Company learned the importance of financial planning in building lasting wealth. The financial planner assesses the company's financial situation, including its income, expenses, debts, and cash flow. They also discuss the company's short-term and long-term financial goals.

Based on this analysis, the financial planner creates a comprehensive financial plan for ABC Construction Company. The plan includes a budgeting strategy to control expenses, a debt repayment plan, and a cash flow management plan to ensure that the company has adequate cash reserves to cover its expenses and invest in growth opportunities.

The financial planner also recommends that ABC Construction Company diversify its services and expand its customer base to reduce its reliance on a few key clients. They also advise the company to improve its marketing strategy and increase its online presence to attract more clients.

ABC Construction Company starts implementing the financial planner's recommendations, which require some changes to their business strategy and operations. They implement cost-cutting measures, renegotiate contracts with suppliers, and improve their billing and collection processes. They also invest in training their employees to improve their skills and provide better-quality services to clients.

Over the years, ABC Construction Company has stuck to its financial plan and adjusted it as necessary to accommodate changes in the business environment. The company starts to see positive results, with improved cash flow, profitability, and growth opportunities.

By the time ABC Construction Company reaches its 10th anniversary, it will have become a leading provider of construction services in the local area. The company has diversified its services, expanded its customer base, and has a strong online presence that attracts new clients. It has also built a comfortable financial cushion and invested in growth opportunities that have paid off in the long run.

This case study demonstrates the importance of financial planning in building lasting wealth for struggling businesses. By taking control of their finances, seeking professional advice, and implementing a comprehensive financial plan, ABC Construction Company was able to turn their business around, achieve their financial goals, and build lasting wealth for their future.

Driving Success: Nasrudeen Mohamed's Journey

Nasrudeen Mohamed, founder of Jumbo Jet Auto Sales, has defied the odds and built a thriving automotive business in Guyana. From humble beginnings, he has grown his business into a leading provider of affordable, high-quality vehicles. But what has contributed to his remarkable success? Nasrudeen Mohamed has a well-defined business strategy that has enabled him to build a strong brand and expand his business. He recognized the demand for affordable, high-quality vehicles in Guyana and positioned Jumbo Jet Auto Sales as a leading provider of such vehicles. He also implemented a customer-focused strategy, providing excellent customer service and ensuring that his customers were satisfied with their purchases.

Jumbo Jet Auto Sales offers competitive pricing on its vehicles, which has helped the company attract and retain customers. Nasrudeen Mohamed has leveraged his relationships with suppliers to negotiate favorable prices and has passed on these savings to his customers.

Nasrudeen Mohamed has diversified his business to include other services, such as vehicle financing and servicing. This has helped him capture more market share and provide a one-stop shop for customers looking to purchase and maintain their vehicles.

Jumbo Jet Auto Sales has a strong marketing strategy that has helped to increase brand awareness and attract new customers. Nasrudeen Mohamed has leveraged social media and other digital marketing channels to reach a wider audience and promote his business.

LO2: Money Matters Made Simple: Overcoming Common Obstacles

As entrepreneurs embark on their journey to build successful businesses, they often encounter various financial obstacles and challenges that can hinder their progress. However, with the right strategies and tools, these challenges can be overcome, and entrepreneurs can achieve financial success. Below, we will explore some strategies to overcome common financial obstacles and challenges.

One of the most important strategies for small business owners is to **have a solid financial plan in plac**e. This includes setting financial goals, creating a budget, and tracking expenses and revenues. By having a clear understanding of their financial situation and goals, small business owners can make informed decisions about their business, prioritize spending, and avoid overspending. For example, a small business owner who wants to expand their business may set a financial goal to save a certain amount of money each month for a year to fund the expansion. By creating a budget and tracking expenses, they can identify areas where they can cut costs and save money, such as by reducing unnecessary expenses or negotiating better prices with vendors.

Another strategy that small business owners can use is to **leverage technology to manage their finances more efficiently.** For example, using accounting software like QuickBooks or Xero can help small business owners track their expenses and revenues, generate financial reports, and manage cash flow. By using technology, small business owners can save time and reduce the risk of errors, allowing them to focus on other aspects of their business. Additionally, there are numerous financial apps available that can help small business owners with tasks such as invoicing, payroll, and budgeting.

A third strategy for small business owners is to **diversify their revenue streams**. This can help reduce the risk of relying on a single source of income and make the business more resilient in the face of economic challenges. For example, a small business owner who runs a coffee shop may also offer catering services or sell merchandise, such as branded mugs or t-shirts. By diversifying their revenue streams, the business owner can generate additional income and create new opportunities for growth.

A fourth strategy for small business owners is to **build strong relationships with their customers and vendors**. This can help to create a loyal customer base and negotiate better prices with vendors, which can reduce expenses and improve cash flow. For example, a small business owner who runs a boutique clothing store may offer personalized styling services to their customers, creating a strong relationship and repeat business. Similarly, they may negotiate with their vendors to receive better prices on their products, which can help reduce expenses and increase profits.

Additional Strategies for Financial Success

Debt

Debt can be a significant burden for entrepreneurs, potentially restricting their ability to grow their businesses and achieve profitability. It can stem from sources such as business loans, credit card debt, or personal financial obligations. Overcoming this obstacle requires entrepreneurs to employ the following strategies:

Debt restructuring and consolidation: Exploring options to consolidate high-interest debt or renegotiating repayment terms can alleviate the burden and improve cash flow.

Creating a debt repayment plan: Developing a comprehensive plan to prioritize and systematically pay off debts allows entrepreneurs to regain control over their finances and reduce interest expenses.

Improving cash flow management: Implementing strategies such as tightening credit policies, optimizing inventory management, and negotiating better terms with suppliers can help improve cash flow and alleviate the burden of debt.

Case Study: Debt Recovery and Consolidation for a Small Retail Business

Sarah's business faced a difficult period due to unforeseen circumstances, and she accumulated significant debt from various sources, including business loans and credit card balances. The burden of high-interest debt was affecting her cash flow and hindering her ability to invest in growth opportunities. To overcome this challenge, Sarah decided to pursue debt recovery and consolidation strategies.

Assessing the debt situation: Sarah first assessed her total outstanding debt, including the amounts owed, interest rates, and repayment terms for each debt source. This evaluation provided her with a clear picture of the extent of her debt and helped her prioritize her repayment strategy.

Negotiating with creditors: Sarah reached out to her creditors, including banks and credit card companies, to discuss possible debt restructuring options. She explained her financial situation honestly and requested more favorable terms, such as reduced interest rates or extended repayment periods. By negotiating with her creditors, Sarah aimed to alleviate the burden of high-interest debt and improve her cash flow.

Consolidating debts: After evaluating her options, Sarah decided to pursue debt consolidation as a means to simplify her repayment process and potentially secure lower interest rates. She applied for a business consolidation loan that would enable her to combine all her high-interest debts into a single, more manageable loan. This consolidation loan would ideally have a lower interest rate, offering Sarah the advantage of reduced monthly payments and the ability to pay off her debts faster.

Developing a debt repayment plan: With the consolidation loan approved, Sarah worked with a financial advisor to create a structured debt repayment plan. This plan involved determining a fixed monthly payment that Sarah could comfortably afford while ensuring that she could cover her other business expenses. By adhering to this plan, Sarah aimed to systematically pay off her debts over a specified period.

Improved financial management: Alongside debt recovery and consolidation, Sarah implemented stronger financial management practices to prevent future debt accumulation. She created a comprehensive budget that accounted for all business expenses, prioritized savings, and monitored cash flow closely. Sarah also sought guidance from her financial advisor on effective money management strategies, such as implementing cost-cutting measures and improving inventory management, to optimize her business's financial health.

By pursuing debt recovery and consolidation strategies, Sarah successfully reduced the burden of her debt, improved her cash flow, and regained control over her business finances. With a structured debt repayment plan in place and enhanced financial management practices, Sarah was better positioned to allocate her resources towards business growth and achieve long-term financial stability.

Inadequate Savings

Insufficient savings can hinder an entrepreneur's ability to weather unforeseen challenges and seize growth opportunities. Overcoming this challenge requires entrepreneurs to focus on the following strategies:

Establishing an emergency fund: Building a dedicated fund to cover unexpected expenses or periods of slow business allows entrepreneurs to maintain stability and avoid resorting to debt.

Prioritizing savings in the business budget: Allocating a specific portion of revenue towards savings as a non-negotiable expense reinforces the importance of building a financial safety net.

Seeking alternative funding sources: Exploring options such as angel investors, crowdfunding, or small business grants can provide additional capital and help bridge any gaps in savings.

Poor Money Management

Ineffective money management can undermine an entrepreneur's financial success. Poor budgeting, overspending, and insufficient financial tracking can all contribute to this challenge. Entrepreneurs can overcome poor money management by implementing the following strategies:

Creating a realistic budget: Developing a comprehensive budget that accounts for all business expenses, tracks revenue, and incorporates financial goals enables entrepreneurs to make informed decisions and optimize their financial resources.

Implementing robust bookkeeping systems: Utilizing accounting software or hiring professional bookkeepers ensures accurate financial records and provides visibility into the financial health of the business.

Conducting regular financial reviews: Periodic reviews of financial statements, cash flow, and expense reports enable entrepreneurs to identify inefficiencies and areas for improvement and make necessary adjustments.

Limited Financial Knowledge

Insufficient financial knowledge can hinder entrepreneurs' ability to make sound financial decisions, understand complex financial concepts, and seize opportunities for growth. To overcome this challenge, entrepreneurs can consider the following strategies:

Self-education: Actively seeking knowledge through books, online resources, and industry-specific financial publications allows entrepreneurs to enhance their financial literacy and make informed decisions.

Engaging with mentors or advisors: Seeking guidance from experienced mentors or financial advisors can provide valuable insights, help navigate complex financial situations, and bridge knowledge gaps.

Networking and industry involvement: Participating in industry conferences, workshops, and networking events exposes entrepreneurs to experts who can share financial insights and best practices.

In conclusion, small business owners face many financial obstacles and challenges, but with the right strategies and tools, they can overcome them and achieve financial success. By creating a solid financial plan, leveraging technology, diversifying revenue streams, and building strong relationships with customers and vendors, small business owners can navigate the complex world of business finances and thrive. As the saying goes, "failing to plan is planning to fail," and this is particularly true when it comes to small business finances. By taking proactive steps to manage their finances, small business owners can build a strong and successful business that will stand the test of time.

LO3: Opportunity Navigator

Entrepreneurship is a journey that encompasses not only the pursuit of passion and innovation but also the desire to generate income and build wealth. As an aspiring or established entrepreneur, one of your key learning objectives should be to identify opportunities that can help you increase your income and pave the way towards long-term financial success. We will explore various strategies and insights to assist you in recognizing and capitalizing on these opportunities. Here are some strategies:

Understanding the Market

The first step in identifying income-boosting opportunities is to have a deep understanding of the market you operate in. Conduct thorough market research to identify current trends, consumer demands, and potential gaps. By understanding the needs and pain points of your target audience, you can develop innovative solutions that have the potential to generate substantial income.

Embrace Innovation

Innovation is a powerful tool for entrepreneurs seeking to increase their income and build wealth. Stay updated on technological advancements, emerging industries, and disruptive business models. Innovation can help you create unique products or services that address unmet needs or provide a competitive edge. Explore opportunities for process optimization, automation, and leveraging cutting-edge technologies to enhance efficiency and drive profitability.

Developing Multiple Revenue Streams

One of the most effective ways to increase income and build wealth as an entrepreneur is to develop multiple revenue streams. This can be done by diversifying your product or service offerings or expanding your target market. For example, a bakery that specializes in custom cakes can also offer cupcakes and cookies to attract more customers and increase revenue.

Scaling the Business

Another way to increase income and build wealth as an entrepreneur is to scale the business. Increasing production or expanding operations to reach new markets can accomplish this. For example, a clothing store can open new locations in different cities or expand its online presence to reach customers in other countries.

Investing in Real Estate

Investing in real estate can be a lucrative opportunity to build wealth as an entrepreneur. You can achieve this by buying properties to rent out or flipping them for a profit. For example, a real estate investor can purchase a property in a desirable location, renovate it, and sell it for a higher price.

Leveraging Technology

Technology can be a powerful tool for entrepreneurs to increase income and build wealth. This can be done by creating an online platform or leveraging social media to reach a wider audience. For example, a personal trainer can create an online course or membership program to offer their services to people all over the world.

Developing a Strong Brand

Developing a strong brand can help entrepreneurs increase their income and build wealth by attracting more customers and commanding higher prices. This can be achieved by creating a unique brand identity, offering high-quality products or services, and providing exceptional customer service. For example, a luxury jewelry brand can charge premium prices for their products by creating a brand that is associated with quality and exclusivity.

In summary, there are several opportunities for entrepreneurs to increase their income and build wealth. Whether it's developing multiple revenue streams, scaling the business, investing in real estate, leveraging technology, or developing a strong brand, entrepreneurs can take advantage of these strategies to achieve financial success. However, it's important to remember that building wealth takes time, patience, and perseverance, and success is not guaranteed.

Intellectual property: A window of opportunity

Intellectual property (IP) refers to intangible creations of the human intellect, such as inventions, literary and artistic works, designs, symbols, names, and images used in commerce. It can be a valuable asset for entrepreneurs, offering significant opportunities to increase income and build wealth. Below are some ways in which intellectual property can benefit entrepreneurs.

Protection and Exclusivity

By securing intellectual property rights, entrepreneurs can protect their innovative ideas, inventions, and creations from unauthorized use or replication by others. Patents, trademarks, and copyrights provide legal protection, granting exclusivity to the owner and preventing competitors from profiting from their intellectual assets. This exclusivity can create a competitive advantage and enable entrepreneurs to capitalize on their creations without undue competition, thus increasing their income potential.

Revenue Generation through Licensing

Intellectual property can be licensed to other businesses or individuals, allowing them to use the protected creations in exchange for licensing fees or royalties. This enables entrepreneurs to generate passive income streams without the need for extensive manufacturing, distribution, or marketing efforts. Licensing agreements can provide a consistent revenue stream while leveraging the reputation and market demand for intellectual property.

Branding and Brand Equity

Trademarks, logos, and brand names are essential elements of intellectual property that contribute to the overall value of a brand. Building a strong brand through intellectual property can establish customer loyalty, trust, and recognition in the marketplace. A well-established brand can command higher prices for products or services, attract more customers, and increase market share, leading to increased income and long-term wealth creation.

Strategic Partnerships and Joint Ventures

Intellectual property can be a catalyst for forging strategic partnerships and joint ventures. Businesses with valuable intellectual assets can enter into collaborations with other companies, combining their resources, expertise, and market reach. These partnerships can lead to new market opportunities, expanded distribution channels, and increased revenue potential. Joint ventures can also facilitate shared research and development efforts, leading to innovative breakthroughs and intellectual property expansion.

Expansion into New Markets

Intellectual property can open doors to new markets and expansion opportunities. Entrepreneurs can license or franchise their intellectual property rights to local partners or businesses in different geographic regions. This allows them to enter new markets with minimal investment and leverage the local market knowledge and infrastructure of their partners. Expanding into new markets diversifies revenue streams, broadens the customer base, and provides avenues for increased income and wealth accumulation.

Valuable Asset for Financing and Exit Strategies

Intellectual property adds tangible value to a business, making it an attractive asset for financing or investment. Investors and lenders recognize the potential of intellectual property to generate revenue and create a competitive advantage. Intellectual property assets can be leveraged to secure loans, attract venture capital, or negotiate favorable terms in mergers and acquisitions. Entrepreneurs can also consider monetizing their intellectual property through a sale or licensing agreement as part of their exit strategy, providing a significant return on investment and wealth accumulation.

In this chapter, we highlighted the crucial aspects of building a strong financial future and unlocking your wealth mindset. The chapter aimed to help you understand the importance of financial planning, strategies to overcome obstacles, and opportunities to increase income and build wealth. Let's summarize the key takeaways from each learning objective:

We emphasize the significance of financial planning in the pursuit of lasting wealth. A well-crafted financial plan serves as a roadmap for achieving your financial goals and helps you make informed decisions about saving, investing, and spending. Without a plan, you risk falling into financial pitfalls and experiencing undesirable consequences. By understanding the importance of financial planning, you can lay a solid foundation for your financial future.

Financial obstacles and challenges are common on the path to wealth creation. We explored various strategies to overcome these hurdles, such as developing a resilient mindset, practicing effective budgeting, managing debt wisely, and building an emergency fund. By adopting proactive financial habits and implementing strategies to overcome obstacles, you can navigate the challenges and move closer to your financial goals.

We highlighted the significance of understanding the market, embracing innovation, diversifying revenue streams, leveraging technology, capitalizing on emerging trends, and engaging in continuous learning. By recognizing and capitalizing on these opportunities, entrepreneurs can unlock new avenues for financial success and long-term wealth creation.

Building a strong financial future requires a holistic approach that encompasses financial planning, overcoming obstacles, and identifying opportunities. It demands a proactive mindset, financial discipline, and the willingness to take calculated risks. As Nelson Mandela rightly said, "There is no passion in settling for a life that is less than the one you are capable of living." By implementing the knowledge gained from this chapter and nurturing your wealth mindset, you can pave the way for a future of financial prosperity and fulfillment. In the next chapter, we will explore building and leveraging relationships.

CHAPTER 7

Building and Leveraging Relationships for Financial Success

Even the lone ranger didn't do it alone.
—**Harvey MacKay**

Learning Objectives

This chapter will help you understand the following factors that are critical to unlocking your wealth mindset:

> **LO1:** Identify the importance of networking and relationship-building in business and finance.

> **LO2:** Develop effective communication and negotiation skills to establish and nurture relationships with stakeholders.

> **LO3:** Build a supportive community and leverage resources for success.

Forging Connections: The Potency of Relationships

In addition to one's own abilities, connections are also important to success. Networking and relationship-building have emerged as quintessential elements for business owners, acting as conduits to growth, opportunities, and financial prosperity.

Caribbean Delight is a popular restaurant chain with locations across the region. They understand that building strong networks and relationships is crucial for their success in the competitive business landscape. The company actively engages in networking activities, both within the food industry and with potential partners and stakeholders in finance.

Through networking events, trade shows, and industry conferences, Caribbean Delights establishes connections with suppliers, distributors, and other key players in the food and beverage sector. By cultivating these relationships, the company ensures a steady supply of high-quality ingredients, favorable pricing, and access to the latest food trends. These networks also provide opportunities for collaboration, such as joint marketing initiatives and cross-promotions, which help expand the brand's reach and attract a wider customer base.

Caribbean Delights also recognizes the significance of networking in the financial aspect of its operations. The company actively seeks relationships with financial institutions, investors, and lenders to secure the necessary capital for expansion, new store openings, and equipment upgrades. By establishing trust and credibility through networking, Caribbean Delights gains access to favorable financing terms, strategic financial advice, and potential investment opportunities.

The restaurant chain leverages relationships with business associations, tourism boards, and local communities to enhance its visibility and reputation. Caribbean Delights actively participates in community events, sponsors local initiatives, and forms partnerships with regional organizations. These relationships not only contribute to the brand's positive image but also attract tourists, boost customer loyalty, and generate valuable word-of-mouth marketing.

Caribbean Delights' success can be attributed to its understanding of the importance of networking and relationship-building in both the culinary and financial realms. By actively fostering connections, the company has been able to secure reliable suppliers, access favorable financing, and strengthen its brand presence in the region. Through strategic networking efforts, Caribbean Delights has established itself as a thriving business in the Caribbean, serving as an inspiration for other entrepreneurs who recognize the power of networking and relationship-building in achieving business and financial success.

LO1: Value of Networking and Relationships

There are significant benefits that can be leveraged through networking and relationship-building. Here are some values to be considered:

Gateway to Opportunities

Networking serves as a gateway to a realm of endless possibilities. By actively engaging with like-minded individuals, industry professionals, and potential partners, business owners can unlock a treasure trove of opportunities that may otherwise remain hidden. Opportunities can manifest in various forms, such as strategic alliances, joint ventures, collaborations, or access to capital. Those who actively network position themselves favorably to seize the opportunities that drive their businesses towards exponential growth in a world where connections are everything.

A Tapestry of Trust

Relationship-building forms the very fabric upon which businesses thrive. Trust lies at the heart of successful relationships, serving as the adhesive that cements partnerships and fosters collaboration. When business owners invest time and effort in building meaningful connections, they cultivate an environment where trust is nurtured. Such trust paves the way for enhanced cooperation, shared knowledge, and mutual support, ultimately laying the foundation for long-term success. In the realm of finance, trust is often the catalyst that allows business owners to secure favorable terms, attract investors, and navigate complex financial landscapes.

Amplifying Influence

Networking and relationship-building provide a platform to amplify one's influence and establish a powerful presence within the business community. By connecting with influential individuals and thought leaders, business owners can tap into a wealth of knowledge, industry insights, and cutting-edge trends. Moreover, by positioning themselves as reliable and trustworthy professionals, entrepreneurs can establish their brand as an industry authority. Through strategic networking, business owners can harness the power of influence to enhance their reputation, attract high-value clients, and propel their financial success to new heights.

Knowledge Sharing and Collaborative Learning

Knowledge exchange and collaborative learning are the pillars of a prosperous and interconnected business environment. By participating in networks and cultivating meaningful relationships, business owners can create a dynamic ecosystem that fosters the exchange of knowledge, ideas, and insights. This collaborative environment affords endless opportunities for development and enhancement.

Entrepreneurs have the opportunity to interact with colleagues, industry experts, and seasoned mentors within these networks. These interactions provide fertile ground for discussions on a variety of business issues, strategies, and emerging trends. Individuals can obtain invaluable advice and feedback through the lens of shared experiences, enabling them to make more informed decisions.

The process of collaborative learning extends beyond the passive assimilation of information. Instead, it encourages participation and active engagement. As business proprietors share their own experiences and insights, they enrich the community as a whole by contributing to the body of collective knowledge. This virtuous cycle fosters a supportive and nurturing environment in which everyone benefits from the group's collective intelligence.

Weathering Storms and Overcoming Challenges

In today's dynamic business world, storms and difficulties are inherent in the journey. However, entrepreneurs who develop a robust network and cultivate strong relationships can withstand these storms with greater confidence and tenacity. During times of turmoil, the significance of a supportive network becomes especially apparent as it serves as a lifeline, providing essential resources and fortifying resilience.

Diversity is at the core of any worthwhile network. By cultivating relationships with people from diverse backgrounds, industries, and areas of expertise, business proprietors gain access to a vast array of perspectives and insights. A diverse network provides entrepreneurs with access to a larger reservoir of knowledge and problem-solving strategies, enabling them to confront challenges from multiple angles.

Within this network, mentoring emerges as a valuable asset. Mentors who have overcome adversity themselves can provide guidance and insight to those facing similar obstacles. Their tales of overcoming adversity can serve as beacons of hope and inspiration, imparting a sense that obstacles can be overcome. In times of crisis, mentors can provide entrepreneurs with tailored advice and direction, enabling them to make informed decisions and navigate uncertain terrain.

From Island Charm to Global Success

In the captivating Caribbean Islands, where sun-drenched beaches meet vibrant cultures, a remarkable business emerged that exemplified the power of effective communication and negotiation. This true story chronicles the journey of a small Caribbean company that transformed itself into a global success by skillfully establishing and nurturing relationships with stakeholders through these essential skills.

The idyllic island of St. Lucia, where a passionate entrepreneur named Maria embarked on her dream of opening a boutique resort Maria's vision was to offer an immersive, culturally rich experience to her guests. However, she quickly realized that success hinged not only on providing a beautiful resort but also on building strong relationships with stakeholders.

Maria understood the importance of effective communication from the start. She engaged with local suppliers, craftsmen, and tour operators, immersing herself in the island's culture and fostering genuine connections. By listening attentively and adapting her communication style to match the locals' warm and relaxed manner, Maria built trust and established a loyal network of stakeholders. Her dedication to effective negotiation ensured fair and mutually beneficial agreements, securing reliable suppliers and partners.

Maria set her sights on going beyond the local market as a result of her early success. She recognized the need to develop her communication and negotiation skills to navigate the complexities of the global business landscape. She sought opportunities to enhance her knowledge, attending workshops and conferences to learn from industry experts and fellow entrepreneurs.

Equipped with newfound insights, Maria embraced digital platforms and social media to connect with potential international partners and guests. Her ability to adapt her communication style to different cultures and languages allowed her to foster relationships with stakeholders from diverse backgrounds. Through active listening and understanding their unique needs, Maria nurtured these relationships, ensuring that her business thrived on global platforms.

As Maria's business grew, she encountered various challenges along the way. However, her effective communication and negotiation skills became invaluable assets in overcoming these obstacles. During times of economic downturn, Maria engaged in open and honest conversations with stakeholders, demonstrating her commitment to collaboration and finding mutually beneficial solutions.

Maria recognized the importance of consistent relationship maintenance. She invested time and effort in staying connected with her stakeholders, reaching out regularly, and seeking feedback. Through proactive communication and feedback loops, Maria continually refined her services and adapted to changing market demands. This commitment to constant improvement allowed her business to remain resilient and continue its upward trajectory.

Maria's journey serves as an inspiring testament to the transformative power of effective communication and negotiation in business. From humble beginnings in the Caribbean, her commitment to building relationships and nurturing stakeholders propelled her business to international acclaim. By embracing the principles of active listening, cultural adaptation, and win-win negotiations, Maria established a global network of partners, suppliers, and customers.

This demonstrates that even in a small island paradise, businesses can achieve remarkable success by developing effective communication and negotiation skills. The lessons learned from Maria's journey remind us that the foundation of sustainable growth lies in establishing genuine connections, fostering trust, and nurturing relationships with stakeholders. Through these skills, businesses in the Caribbean and beyond can overcome challenges, seize opportunities, and create a lasting impact on a global scale.

LO2: Enhance Communication and Negotiation for Lasting Connections

The ability to establish and nurture relationships with stakeholders is paramount to achieving long-term success. Effective communication and negotiation skills form the foundation for fostering these relationships. By mastering these skills, businesses can enhance collaboration, build trust, and create mutually beneficial outcomes. There are different ways businesses can develop effective communication and negotiation skills that can help establish and nurture relationships with stakeholders.

1. Establish Trust through Effective Communication

Effective communication serves as the cornerstone for building trust with stakeholders. Businesses must strive for clarity, transparency, and active listening in their interactions. By clearly conveying their objectives, values, and expectations, businesses can establish a common ground and align stakeholders' interests with their own. Regular and open communication channels create an environment of trust and promote collaboration.

2. Active Listening and Understanding Stakeholder Needs

Active listening is a critical aspect of effective communication. By attentively listening to stakeholders' concerns, needs, and aspirations, businesses can gain valuable insights into their expectations.

Understanding stakeholder perspectives allows businesses to tailor their communication and negotiation strategies accordingly. This empathetic approach demonstrates that the business values the stakeholders' input, which strengthens the relationship.

3. Negotiation Skills for Win-Win Outcomes

Negotiation skills play a pivotal role in creating mutually beneficial outcomes for both businesses and stakeholders. Effective negotiation involves understanding the interests and objectives of all parties involved. By adopting a collaborative mindset, businesses can explore creative solutions that address stakeholders' needs while aligning with their own goals. Skilled negotiators focus on building rapport, seeking common ground, and finding win-win scenarios that promote long-term relationships.

4. Adapting to Diverse Stakeholder Communication Styles

In a diverse business environment, stakeholders may come from various backgrounds and have different communication styles. Businesses must adapt their communication approach to effectively engage with different stakeholders. Flexibility in communication enables businesses to build rapport and establish rapport with stakeholders from different cultures, generations, or industries. By recognizing and respecting these differences, businesses can foster stronger relationships and better collaboration.

5. Consistent relationship maintenance

Establishing relationships with stakeholders is an ongoing process that requires consistent effort and maintenance. Businesses must nurture these relationships beyond transactional interactions. Regular communication, follow-ups, and demonstrating continued value are vital to maintaining strong stakeholder relationships. Businesses should also seek feedback to continuously improve their communication and negotiation strategies, ensuring alignment with stakeholders' evolving needs.

Effective communication and negotiation skills are indispensable tools for businesses to establish and nurture relationships with stakeholders. By actively listening, empathizing, and adapting communication styles, businesses can foster trust, understanding, and collaboration. Skilled negotiators aim for win-win outcomes that satisfy both business objectives and stakeholder interests. Cultivating these skills is an ongoing process that requires consistent effort and a genuine commitment to building strong, lasting relationships. Ultimately, businesses that prioritize effective communication and negotiation will thrive in establishing meaningful connections with their stakeholders, fostering mutual growth and success.

LO3: Community Powerhouse: Harnessing Collective Resources for Lasting Success

Success is not achieved in isolation. It is crucial for business professionals to build a supportive community and leverage available resources to unlock their full potential. Building a supportive community is important to cultivate a strong network, and harnessing resources is an essential strategy for achieving success in the business world. Through examples and practical insights, we will uncover the benefits and practical steps to building a supportive community and leveraging resources effectively.

Supportive Community

The development and maintenance of a supportive community are crucial to achieving business success. A network of similar individuals, colleagues, mentors, and customers can offer invaluable resources, guidance, and encouragement. Let's examine some compelling examples that illustrate the importance of establishing and sustaining a supportive community for entrepreneurial success in this context.

Mentorship and Guidance

Within a supportive community, seasoned entrepreneurs frequently serve as mentors, guiding and advising newcomers based on their own experiences. This guidance can be invaluable for avoiding common pitfalls, making intelligent decisions, and navigating uncharted territory. In order to benefit from the knowledge and insights of those who have already found success, mentorship programs, seminars, and networking opportunities within the community can foster these relationships.

Networking and Collaboration

Within a hospitable community, collaboration becomes a primary motivator. Entrepreneurs can find potential partners whose skills and offerings complement their own, resulting in collaborative ventures, partnerships, and the co-creation of products and services. Collaborations of this nature not only expand the scope of their enterprises but also provide access to new markets and customers. By combining their resources and knowledge, community members can undertake ambitious initiatives that would be impossible on their own.

Emotional Support and Motivation

Uncertainty and setbacks are frequently a part of entrepreneurship and business ventures. A supportive community provides emotional support during challenging times, fosters resilience, and keeps motivation high. It is invaluable to surround yourself with people who understand your journey and can provide support when it is required. This emotional support enables entrepreneurs to remain resilient and persistent in the face of adversity. When a business owner feels disheartened, the community's uplifting words and encouragement can reignite their passion and resolve to move forward.

Leveraging Resources

A supportive community provides a rich resource pool that can significantly impact a business's success. This resource sharing can encompass tangible assets like funding, equipment, or office space as well as intangible resources such as skills, knowledge, and contacts. Start-ups, especially those with limited capital, can greatly benefit from collaborating with other members to achieve collective goals. For example, entrepreneurs might collaborate on joint projects, share supplier contacts, or co-host events, amplifying the impact of their individual efforts and reducing costs.

Financial Resources

Access to capital is crucial for business growth and sustainability. Entrepreneurs can leverage resources such as venture capital firms, government grants, crowdfunding platforms, or even angel investors to secure the necessary funding for their ventures.

Knowledge and Expertise

In the rapidly changing environment of the information age, the acquisition and application of knowledge and expertise have become essential for business professionals pursuing success in their respective fields. Business professionals can utilize online courses, webinars, podcasts, and industry-specific publications to hone their skills and remain informed of the most recent developments. In addition, collaborating with specialists or consultants can provide specialized knowledge and unique perspectives in areas where additional expertise is required.

In today's business environment, successful professionals cannot afford the danger of complacency. Organizations develop a growth mindset when they embrace a culture of continuous improvement and invest in knowledge acquisition. Individuals are more likely to innovate, experiment, and promote positive change when they are encouraged and supported in their pursuit of knowledge. This culture of learning fosters innovation and flexibility, enabling business professionals to seize new opportunities and overcome obstacles with fortitude.

Technology and Tools

Implementing technology and tools can substantially streamline a variety of business processes, resulting in increased efficiency and decreased operational overhead. Automation is crucial to attaining this goal. Using robotic process automation (RPA), repetitive tasks can be automated, which frees up employees' time and resources to concentrate on more strategic and creative aspects of their jobs. In addition, integrated systems and software platforms enable seamless data transmission across departments, thereby minimizing bottlenecks and errors. As a result, businesses can operate more efficiently, respond more quickly to challenges, and provide products or services with greater consistency and dependability.

The digital revolution has provided businesses with a vast array of technological resources and tools. From customer relationship management (CRM) software to cloud computing solutions, leveraging technology can streamline operations, enhance productivity, and facilitate better decision-making.

In Summary, Building a supportive community and leveraging available resources are critical components of achieving success in the business world. By cultivating relationships, seeking mentorship, and actively participating in networking opportunities, professionals can tap into a community that offers guidance, collaboration, and motivation. Simultaneously, recognizing and utilizing available resources such as financial support, knowledge, and technology empowers individuals to unlock their full potential. By combining these strategies, business professionals can navigate challenges, seize opportunities, and achieve sustainable success in an increasingly competitive environment. Remember, success is rarely a solo endeavor; it is the result of collective support and resourcefulness.

In this chapter, we explored three critical factors that are essential for unlocking a wealth mindset: networking and relationship-building, effective communication and negotiation skills, and building a supportive community.

It highlighted the importance of networking and relationship-building in the realms of business and finance. We recognized that success in these fields often hinges on the connections we make and nurture. By actively engaging in networking opportunities, we can expand our professional network, create collaborative partnerships, and gain access to valuable resources and opportunities.

The next chapter focused on developing effective communication and negotiation skills to establish and nurture relationships with stakeholders. We learned that clear and concise communication, active listening, and the ability to articulate our ideas and goals are crucial for building strong connections. Additionally, we discovered the power of negotiation in building mutually beneficial relationships, enabling us to achieve win-win outcomes and build trust with stakeholders.

The final learning objective emphasized the importance of building a supportive community and leveraging resources for success. We recognized that no one achieves success in isolation, and having a supportive network can provide invaluable guidance, mentorship, and encouragement. By actively seeking out like-minded individuals, participating in communities of practice, and leveraging available resources, we can enhance our chances of achieving our goals and unlocking our wealth mindset.

By understanding and applying these strategies and tools, we can cultivate a mindset that is conducive to wealth creation and financial success. By recognizing the significance of networking and relationship-building, developing effective communication and negotiation skills, and building a supportive community, we position ourselves to seize opportunities, leverage resources, and overcome challenges on our journey towards financial abundance.

Practical Activity: Building Your Wealth Network

Objective: To apply the concepts and skills learned in this chapter by actively engaging in networking and relationship-building activities to develop a wealth mindset.

Guidelines:

Step 1: Identify a Networking Event

Research and find a networking event or business gathering in your local area that aligns with your interests or career aspirations. Look for events related to finance, entrepreneurship, or any other field you are passionate about.

Step 2: Prepare for the Networking Event

a) Review the key communication and negotiation skills discussed in the chapter.

b) Create a personal elevator pitch that succinctly describes who you are, what you do, and what you are looking to achieve in your career or business.

c) Prepare a set of open-ended questions to ask others during the event to facilitate meaningful conversations and demonstrate your interest in their work or interests. (example:Tell me about your relationship with your team.)

Step 3: Attend the Networking Event

a) Dress professionally and arrive early to familiarize yourself with the event space.

b) Introduce yourself to at least three new people and engage in conversations using the skills and techniques learned.

c) Use your prepared questions to initiate discussions and listen actively to others' responses.

d) Practice effective communication, including maintaining eye contact, active listening, and demonstrating genuine interest in others.

Step 4: Follow-Up and Relationship Building

a) Collect business cards or contact information from the individuals you connected with during the event.

b) Within 48 hours of the event, send personalized follow-up emails or messages expressing your gratitude for the conversation and your interest in maintaining the connection.

c) Look for opportunities to provide value to your new contacts, such as sharing relevant resources, offering introductions to other professionals, or attending events they may find valuable.

Step 5: Reflect and Evaluate

a) Reflect on your networking experience and the effectiveness of your communication and negotiation skills.

b) Identify any challenges or areas for improvement that you observed during the event.

c) Evaluate the success of your follow-up efforts and consider how you can strengthen and nurture these relationships over time.

Step 6: Develop an Action Plan

a) Based on your reflections and evaluation, create an action plan outlining specific steps you will take to further develop your networking and relationship-building skills.

b) Set measurable goals, such as attending a certain number of networking events per month or establishing regular communication with a certain number of key contacts.

Step 7: Monitor Progress and Adjust

a) Regularly review and track your progress towards achieving your networking goals.

b) Adjust your action plan as needed to address any challenges or leverage new opportunities that arise.

Remember:

By actively participating in this practical activity, you will gain hands-on experience in networking and relationship-building by applying the concepts and skills covered in the chapter. This will contribute to unlocking your wealth mindset by expanding your professional network, creating opportunities for collaboration, and accessing valuable resources and support for your financial success.

CHAPTER 8

Time is Valuable: Boosting Productivity and Time Management Skills

Efficiency is doing things right; effectiveness is doing the right thing. —**Peter Drucker**

Learning Objectives

This chapter will help you understand the following factors that are critical to unlocking your wealth mindset:

> **LO1:** Gain knowledge on the importance of time management for personal and professional success and its impact on productivity.

> **LO2:** Develop strategies for managing interruptions and distractions to maximize productivity and achieve desired outcomes.

> **LO3**: Learn effective strategies for managing work-life balance and avoiding burnout.

Time is an ephemeral entity that slips through our fingers like sand, yet it holds the power to shape our personal and professional destinies. Like a master conductor orchestrating a symphony, time management is the baton that directs our actions, propels our progress, and harmonizes the delicate balance between personal and professional success. In the realm of productivity and overall efficiency, mastering time is not a luxury but an absolute necessity.

Effective time management requires setting clear objectives, identifying priorities, and breaking down tasks into manageable units. It involves creating a schedule or a to-do list, setting deadlines, and estimating the time required to complete each task. Time management also involves minimizing or eliminating time-wasting activities, managing distractions, and optimizing productivity by focusing on high-value tasks.

By effectively managing their time, individuals can engage in activities that promote personal growth, such as pursuing hobbies, maintaining relationships, and investing in self-care. Procrastination and poor time management can lead to missed opportunities, increased stress levels, and a sense of unfulfillment.

Island Tours and Adventures

Island Tours & Adventures is a tour and travel company located in a popular tourist destination in the Caribbean. The company specializes in providing unique and memorable experiences to tourists, showcasing the natural beauty and cultural heritage of the region.

The company effectively manages their time to grow their business through successful strategic planning. They allocate dedicated time to analyze market trends, identify target customers, set goals, and develop a comprehensive business plan. By doing so, they can prioritize their activities and allocate resources efficiently. Island Tours & Adventures has implemented streamlined processes and standardized operating procedures. They have clearly defined roles and responsibilities for their employees, ensuring that everyone knows their tasks and can work cohesively. This reduces confusion, minimizes delays, and optimizes overall operational efficiency.

The company places a strong emphasis on the use of digital tools and software to manage schedules, appointments, and bookings. By implementing an efficient booking system, they can avoid double bookings, utilize their resources optimally, and ensure the smooth operation of tours and activities. Island Tours & Adventures believes in the power of delegation and teamwork. They empower their employees by assigning them specific responsibilities and trusting them to carry out their tasks effectively. This enables the management team to focus on strategic decision-making and business growth. They have integrated online booking platforms and a user-friendly website, allowing customers to book tours and activities conveniently. Additionally, they utilize social media platforms for marketing and communication, reaching a wider audience and increasing brand visibility.

Island Tours & Adventures is committed to continuous improvement. They regularly evaluate their processes, seek feedback from customers, and implement necessary changes. By identifying areas for improvement and making necessary adjustments, they can refine their operations and ensure long-term growth. By effectively managing their time, Island Tours & Adventures can provide exceptional service to their customers, maintain a positive reputation, and expand their business in the competitive Caribbean tourism industry.

LO1: Accelerate Productivity with Time Management

Time management is a critical skill for business owners, as it directly impacts productivity, efficiency, and overall success. Below are several reasons why time management is crucial for entrepreneurs:

Prioritization

Effective time management enables business owners to identify and prioritize tasks based on their importance and urgency. By focusing on high-value activities, business owners can make the most of their limited time and ensure that important tasks are completed in a timely manner. For example, instead of spending excessive time on administrative tasks, business owners can allocate time to activities that have a direct impact on revenue generation or business growth.

Increased productivity

When business owners manage their time effectively, they can maximize their productivity. They can allocate specific time blocks for different tasks, minimize distractions, and maintain a structured work routine. This helps to optimize workflow, reduce procrastination, and accomplish more within a given timeframe. For instance, you can dedicate a focused block of time in the morning for creative work or brainstorming sessions and reserve afternoons for meetings or administrative tasks. By establishing a structured schedule, entrepreneurs can optimize their productivity and ensure that important activities receive adequate attention.

Enhanced decision-making

Time management allows business owners to allocate sufficient time for critical decision-making processes. By understanding deadlines and priorities, they can avoid hasty decisions and take the necessary time to gather information, analyze options, and make informed choices.

Delegation and Outsourcing

Effective time management involves recognizing tasks that can be delegated or outsourced. Entrepreneurs can delegate routine or time-consuming tasks to capable team members, virtual assistants, or external service providers. This allows entrepreneurs to focus on core responsibilities that require their expertise and strategic decision-making. By leveraging the skills and capabilities of others, entrepreneurs can increase overall productivity and efficiency.

Avoid Multitasking

Multitasking can actually hinder productivity and result in lower-quality work. Entrepreneurs who practice effective time management understand the importance of focusing on one task at a time. By concentrating on a single task until completion, they can maintain focus, minimize errors, and achieve better outcomes. For instance, instead of switching between multiple projects simultaneously, entrepreneurs allocate dedicated blocks of time to individual projects, ensuring maximum attention and productivity.

Adaptability and flexibility

The ability to manage time effectively enables business owners to respond quickly to changes and unforeseen circumstances. By having a well-organized schedule, they can adapt their plans and allocate time for new opportunities or unexpected challenges without compromising their existing commitments.

Long-term planning

Time management encourages business owners to think strategically and plan for the long term. By allocating time for goal-setting, strategic planning, and reviewing progress, they can steer their business in the desired direction and achieve long-term success.

In summary, time management is essential for business owners to enhance productivity, make informed decisions, reduce stress, and create a healthy work-life balance. By effectively managing their time, business owners can optimize their resources, improve efficiency, and increase their chances of achieving their business goals.

Impact on Productivity

Time management directly affects productivity by ensuring that resources, including time, are utilized optimally. When individuals manage their time effectively, they eliminate unnecessary distractions and allocate dedicated periods for focused work. By doing so, they can enhance their concentration, creativity, and problem-solving abilities. Moreover, effective time management facilitates efficient task completion, reducing the chances of unfinished or delayed work. As a result, productivity levels soar, leading to increased output and better performance.

Impact on Overall Efficiency

Efficiency is the outcome of streamlined processes and optimized resource utilization. Time management plays a crucial role in enhancing overall efficiency. It helps individuals identify their most productive hours, enabling them to schedule complex or critical tasks during periods when they are most alert and focused. Moreover, effective time management reduces time wasted on unimportant activities, interruptions, and multitasking. By organizing tasks and setting clear priorities, individuals can accomplish more in less time, resulting in improved overall efficiency.

Time management is a vital skill that influences personal and professional success as well as overall productivity and efficiency. By effectively managing their time, individuals can prioritize their tasks, set achievable goals, and maintain a healthy work-life balance. In the professional realm, time management enhances productivity, minimizes stress, and contributes to a proactive work culture. It enables individuals to optimize their performance and make a significant impact on their organizations. Therefore, individuals and businesses alike must recognize the importance of time management and develop strategies to harness its benefits for sustained success.

LO2: Maximizing Productivity in a Distracted World

Are interruptions and distractions hijacking your productivity and holding you back from achieving your desired outcomes? It's time to break free from the chains of constant interruption and take control of your focus. In today's fast-paced world, where attention is constantly under siege, mastering the art of managing interruptions and distractions is a game-changer. Imagine what you could accomplish if you could reclaim those precious moments of uninterrupted concentration. This learning objective is your ticket to unlocking the secrets of productivity and achieving unparalleled success. Get ready to discover practical strategies that will empower you to navigate through the chaos, maximize your productivity, and ultimately turn your goals into reality. It's time to reclaim your focus and embrace the power of managing interruptions and distractions. Get ready to revolutionize the way you work and excel like never before!

Some strategies to effectively handle interruptions and minimize distractions are specified below.

Prioritize and Plan

Start by prioritizing your tasks and setting clear goals for the day. This will help you stay focused and minimize the impact of interruptions. Create a to-do list or use a productivity tool to organize your tasks in order of importance. By having a plan in place, you can quickly get back on track after an interruption.

Establish Boundaries

Communicate your availability and boundaries to colleagues, employees, or family members. Let them know your preferred times for uninterrupted work. If possible, set up designated "focus" periods where you can work without interruptions. Establishing clear boundaries helps others understand when it's appropriate to interrupt and when it's best to wait.

Utilize Time Blocking

Time blocking involves scheduling specific blocks of time for different tasks or activities. Allocate uninterrupted blocks of time for your most important and demanding work. During these time blocks, turn off notifications, close unnecessary tabs, and focus solely on the task at hand. This technique helps create a structured workflow and reduces the likelihood of distractions.

Minimize Digital Distractions

Digital distractions, such as social media, email notifications, and instant messaging, can significantly impact productivity. Disable or muffle non-essential notifications on your devices. Consider using website-blocking apps or extensions to limit access to distracting websites during work hours. Designate specific times to check emails and messages rather than constantly responding as they arrive.

Create a Productive Workspace

Designate a dedicated workspace that is free from distractions. This could be a separate room, a quiet corner of your office, or even a coworking space. Make sure your workspace is organized, clutter-free, and optimized for productivity. Minimize visual distractions and keep only essential tools and materials within reach.

Practice the Pomodoro Technique

The Pomodoro Technique is a time management method that involves working in short, focused bursts followed by short breaks. Set a timer for 25 minutes and work on a task with full concentration. After the timer goes off, take a 5-minute break. Repeat this cycle four times, and then take a longer break. This technique helps improve focus and productivity while allowing for periodic rest.

Delegate and Outsource

If you find yourself frequently interrupted by tasks that can be delegated or outsourced, consider assigning those tasks to capable team members or outsourcing them to external professionals. By offloading some responsibilities, you can free up more time to focus on critical tasks that require your attention.

Practice Mindfulness and Self-Awareness

Develop mindfulness practices to cultivate self-awareness and improve your ability to manage distractions. When interrupted, take a moment to assess the urgency and importance of the interruption. Being mindful of your own mental state and ability to concentrate will help you make better decisions about whether to address the interruption immediately or defer it.

Remember, managing interruptions and distractions is an ongoing process. It requires discipline, practice, and a commitment to maintaining focus. By implementing these strategies consistently, you can minimize disruptions, increase productivity, and achieve your desired outcomes.

LO3: Mastering Work-Life Balance for Lasting Success

What if you could avoid feeling like you're constantly teetering on the edge of burnout, struggling to find balance between your personal and professional lives? It's time to take control and reclaim your equilibrium. In a world that never stops, finding effective strategies to manage work-life balance and avoid burnout is not just a luxury but a necessity for sustained success and well-being. Imagine a life where you excel in your career without sacrificing your personal relationships, hobbies, and self-care. This learning objective is your guiding light to discovering the secrets of harmonizing your professional aspirations with a fulfilling personal life. Get ready to equip yourself with practical tools and insights that will empower you to navigate the complexities of modern life, maintain a healthy work-life balance, and prevent burnout from derailing your dreams. It's time to unlock a life of fulfillment, achievement, and vitality. Buckle up and embark on this transformative journey to learn effective strategies for managing work-life balance and embracing a life without burnout. Your path to a harmonious and thriving existence begins now.

Striking the Balance

Lisa Lakey is a Caribbean entrepreneur and the founder of a thriving e-commerce company based in Jamaica. Despite the demands of running a successful business, Lakey has prioritized work-life balance and has become a role model for entrepreneurs in the region.

Lakey recognized early on that maintaining a healthy equilibrium between work and personal life was crucial for sustainable success and overall well-being. She implemented several strategies to achieve work-life balance while still driving her business forward.

First, Lakey established clear boundaries between work and personal life. She dedicated specific time slots for work-related tasks and ensured she had designated time for family, self-care, and relaxation. By compartmentalizing her time, she was able to maintain focus and be fully present in each aspect of her life.

Lakey also emphasized the importance of delegation and building a reliable team. She surrounded herself with capable employees who shared her vision and were entrusted with specific responsibilities. By effectively delegating tasks and empowering her team, Lakey was able to reduce her workload and create more time for herself.

Additionally, Lakey implemented technology and automation to streamline business operations. By leveraging digital tools and systems, she optimized efficiency and reduced time-consuming manual processes. This allowed her to have more freedom and flexibility in managing her time and balancing work and personal commitments.to

Lakey actively practiced self-care to nurture her well-being and recharge her energy. She dedicated time to exercise, meditation, and hobbies that brought her joy. Lakey believed that taking care of herself was essential for maintaining productivity, creativity, and a positive mindset.

Through her example, Lakey has demonstrated that work-life balance is attainable even in the fast-paced entrepreneurial world. She has shown that by setting boundaries, delegating effectively, leveraging technology, and prioritizing self-care, entrepreneurs in the Caribbean can build successful businesses while leading fulfilling personal lives.

Lakey's ability to master work-life balance has not only benefited her personally but has also fostered a healthy and productive work environment for her team. Her success serves as an inspiration to aspiring entrepreneurs in the Caribbean, illustrating that it is possible to create a harmonious integration of work and personal life while achieving entrepreneurial goals.

Set Realistic Goals and Expectations

Avoid setting unrealistic expectations for yourself and your business. Set achievable goals and establish a realistic timeline for their completion. Prioritize tasks based on their importance and urgency. Learn to say no to commitments that don't align with your goals or may overload your schedule.

Continual Learning and Growth

Invest in your personal and professional development. Stay updated on industry trends and advancements. Attend workshops, conferences, or training programs to enhance your skills and knowledge. Continuous learning not only keeps you engaged and motivated but also helps you adapt to changing business environments more effectively.

Practice Effective Time Management

Prioritize and manage your time effectively. Identify your most important tasks and tackle them during your peak productivity hours. Use time management techniques like the Eisenhower Matrix, where you categorize tasks based on their urgency and importance. Minimize distractions and avoid multitasking, focusing on one task at a time to increase efficiency.

Foster Flexibility and Work-Life Integration

Embrace the concept of work-life integration, where work and personal life are not separate entities but rather coexist harmoniously. Look for opportunities to integrate work and personal activities. For example, if possible, schedule family activities during work breaks or find ways to incorporate personal interests into your work routine.

Practice Self-Care

Prioritize self-care and make it a non-negotiable part of your routine. Take care of your physical and mental well-being through regular exercise, healthy eating, quality sleep, and relaxation techniques such as meditation or mindfulness. Set aside time for activities that bring you joy and help you recharge, such as hobbies, spending time with loved ones, or practicing mindfulness and meditation.

Communicate and Seek Support

Effective communication is key to maintaining work-life balance. Clearly communicate your needs and expectations to your colleagues, supervisors, and loved ones. Seek support and share responsibilities with your partner, family members, or trusted friends. Cultivate a support network that can provide guidance, understanding, and encouragement. If you feel overwhelmed despite implementing these strategies, don't hesitate to seek professional support. Reach out to a therapist, counselor, or coach who can help you navigate stress and burnout. They can provide valuable insights, coping mechanisms, and strategies tailored to your specific situation.

Regularly Evaluate and Adjust

Work-life balance is not a static state but an ongoing process. Regularly evaluate your priorities, commitments, and boundaries. Assess if you are allocating time and energy in alignment with your goals and values. Adjust your strategies as needed to ensure they continue to support your overall well-being and success.

Remember, mastering work-life balance is a continuous journey that requires conscious effort and occasional adjustments. By implementing these strategies and adopting a proactive mindset, you can create a sustainable balance between your professional and personal lives, leading to lasting success and fulfillment.

Activity: Time Audit and Priority Matrix

Objective: Develop time management skills and prioritize tasks effectively to boost productivity as a business owner.

General Instructions:

Time Audit:

a. Take a day or a week to track how you spend your time as a business owner. Keep a detailed record of your activities throughout the day, noting the duration spent on each task or activity.

b. Categorize your activities into different areas, such as administrative tasks, client meetings, strategic planning, email management, personal time, etc.

Reflection and Analysis:

a. Reflect on your time audit and examine how you allocate your time across different activities.

b. Identify areas where you might be spending excessive time or areas that require more attention and focus.

Priority Matrix:

a. Create a priority matrix with four quadrants: *Important and Urgent, Important but Not Urgent, Not Important but Urgent,* and *Not Important and Not Urgent.*

b. Review your list of activities from the time audit and categorize them into the appropriate quadrant based on their importance and urgency.

Action Plan:

a. Identify the activities in the *Important and Urgent* quadrant that require immediate attention. These are tasks that directly contribute to your business goals and require your immediate focus.

b. Determine strategies for managing interruptions and distractions for these important and urgent tasks. Consider techniques like setting specific time blocks for uninterrupted work, turning off notifications, or delegating non-essential tasks.

c. Assess the activities in the *important but Not Urgent* quadrant and schedule dedicated time for these tasks. These activities may include long-term planning, skill development, or networking. Allocate specific time slots in your schedule to ensure they receive the attention they deserve.

d. Review the activities in the *Not Important but Urgent* quadrant. Evaluate if these tasks can be delegated or eliminated to free up more time for high-priority activities.

e. Identify activities in the *Not Important and Not Urgent* quadrant that can be eliminated or minimized. These are tasks that do not contribute significantly to your business goals or personal well-being.

Implementation:

a. Put your action plan into practice by prioritizing tasks based on their importance and urgency. Use your priority matrix as a guide to allocate time and attention effectively.

b. Regularly review and update your priorities and strategies to adapt to changing circumstances and new opportunities.

By engaging in this time audit and priority matrix activity,entrepreneurs can gain valuable insights into how they spend their time, identify areas for improvement, and develop effective strategies for managing interruptions and distractions. By prioritizing tasks based on their importance and urgency, entrepreneurs can enhance productivity, achieve desired outcomes, and maintain a healthy work-life balance, ultimately leading to lasting success in their entrepreneurial journey.

In this chapter, we identified the significance of time management in both personal and professional success, recognizing its direct impact on productivity. We explore various factors critical to unlocking a wealth mindset and provide strategies for managing interruptions and distractions and achieving desired outcomes. Furthermore, we address the importance of work-life balance and present effective strategies for avoiding burnout.

We emphasize that efficiency, doing things right, and effectiveness, doing the right things, are both vital elements in optimizing time management. By understanding this distinction, individuals can begin to harness the power of their time and direct it towards activities that yield the greatest impact.

We provide insights and strategies to effectively manage these disruptions, enabling individuals to maintain focus and maximize their output. By implementing these strategies, readers will be equipped with the tools necessary to navigate a world filled with constant distractions and stay on track towards achieving their desired outcomes.

Additionally, the chapter addresses the crucial topic of work-life balance. We emphasize the significance of finding equilibrium between professional and personal commitments to lead a fulfilling and sustainable life. Readers will gain insights into the detrimental effects of burnout and the importance of actively managing work-life balance to prevent it. We present effective strategies and techniques for maintaining this balance, allowing individuals to nurture their personal well-being while still achieving their professional goals.

By the end of this chapter, readers will have gained a comprehensive understanding of the importance of time management, the strategies to manage interruptions and distractions, and the significance of work-life balance in avoiding burnout. Armed with this knowledge, individuals will be empowered to make conscious choices, optimize their productivity, and create a harmonious integration of work and personal life, ultimately enhancing their overall success and well-being.

In the next chapter, we will explore the significance of taking action in achieving goals, strategies for building momentum, and habits that support success.

CHAPTER 9

Forward Bound: Building Momentum Towards Greatness

Success is not final; failure is not fatal. It is the courage to continue that counts. —**Winston Churchill**

Learning Objectives

This chapter will help you understand the following factors that are critical to unlocking your wealth mindset:

LO1: Gain knowledge on the significance of taking action in achieving goals.

LO2: Identify effective strategies for building momentum.

LO3: Learn how to create habits that support success.

In a world brimming with potential and untapped opportunities, there exists a transformative force known as momentum—a catalyst that propels us forward, inch by inch, towards the realm of greatness. But only a renewed mindset can unlock the wealth of possibilities that lie within us.

Are you ready to break free from the shackles of complacency and step into a realm of action, progress, and achievement? If so, this chapter will equip you with the essential tools and insights to pave your path towards success.

The first section unveils the profound significance of taking action in pursuit of our goals. Discover how each step we take, no matter how small, holds the power to shape our destiny. Through the exploration of real-life examples and empirical studies, you will gain invaluable knowledge on the transformative impact of proactive engagement.

Building upon this foundation, it empowers you to identify effective strategies for building momentum. Uncover the secret to harnessing the incredible power of consistent, purposeful action. Explore a myriad of techniques and proven methodologies that will propel you forward, even when faced with daunting challenges.

But it doesn't stop there. We understand that lasting success rests on our habits. Hence, the final section is dedicated to unraveling the art of creating habits that support and sustain triumph. Delve into the psychology behind habit formation and learn how to cultivate behaviors that pave the way for perpetual growth and achievement.

Readers will gain valuable insights to unlock their untapped potential, harness the might of action, and forge habits that will drive them towards unparalleled success. Are you ready to embark on this transformative journey? Prepare to leap forward and seize the greatness that awaits you.

From Trading Goods to Empires: The Chetram Brothers' Journey

There were three brothers in a small village,namely Rory, Amar, and Narrad Chetram. They had lost their mom early in their lives, and coming from a humble background, they had big dreams of creating a prosperous future for themselves and their families. Determined to turn their aspirations into reality, they embarked on a journey filled with challenges, learning opportunities, and remarkable success.

The Chetram brothers knew that knowledge and action were essential to achieving their goals. They began by immersing themselves in books, learning about various industries and business strategies. They understood that taking action was the key to translating their knowledge into tangible outcomes. With a burning desire to succeed, Rory and Amar started trading goods in their village, leveraging their keen business instincts and building a loyal customer base.

As they gained experience and saved their earnings, the brothers identified an opportunity to expand their business and build momentum. They noticed a growing demand for timber in nearby towns and realized that establishing a sawmill could be a game-changer. With their newfound understanding, they took a leap of faith, investing their savings and procuring the necessary equipment.

To build momentum, Rory and Amar implemented effective strategies. They built strong relationships with local timber suppliers, ensuring a steady supply of raw materials. They invested in skilled labor and modern machinery to enhance productivity and quality. They also explored innovative marketing techniques, showcasing their high-quality timber products to potential customers and garnering positive word-of-mouth.

As their sawmill business thrived, the Chetram brothers recognized the need to create habits that supported their continued success. They fostered a culture of discipline, hard work, and continuous improvement within their company. Rory and Amar led by example, working diligently and instilling a strong work ethic in their employees. They encouraged regular training sessions to upgrade skills and implemented robust quality control measures to ensure customer satisfaction.

As their reputation grew, the Chetram brothers expanded their business empire. They diversified into other industries such as medical supplies, real estate, construction, and manufacturing. With each new venture, they applied the same principles they had learned along the way. They sought knowledge, took calculated risks, and built momentum through strategic partnerships and effective execution.

Over the years, the Chetram brothers' group of companies became widely recognized and admired for their success. Their commitment to learning, taking action, and building habits that supported success propelled them to new heights. They became pillars of their community, providing employment opportunities and contributing to the local economy.

While they enjoyed their achievements, the brothers never forgot their humble beginnings. They remained grounded and committed to giving back. They established educational scholarships for underprivileged students, funded community development projects, and mentored aspiring entrepreneurs.

The story of the Chetram brothers is evident in the power of knowledge, action, and habits in achieving extraordinary success. Their journey from trading goods to owning a group of companies showcased how the application of these learning objectives transformed their lives and allowed them to create a lasting impact on their community. Rory and Amar's story serves as an inspiration for generations to come, demonstrating that with determination, resilience, and the right mindset, dreams can indeed become reality.

LO1: The Key to Goal Attainment

In the pursuit of personal and professional success, we often find ourselves enchanted by dreams and aspirations, envisioning a future filled with accomplishments. However, it is through action, the catalyst of progress, that these dreams really come to life. Taking action is the cornerstone of achieving goals, as it propels us forward, transforms mere intentions into tangible results, and bridges the gap between aspiration and reality. Action is being defined as

A - Active engagement in the present moment

C - Courage to take risks and overcome fears

T - Tenacity to persevere and achieve goals

I - Initiative to take charge and make things happen

O - Openness to new ideas and perspectives

N - Never giving up on what truly matters

This section focuses on the significance of actively engaging in tasks and initiatives, illuminating the profound connection between action and goal attainment. By comprehending this vital link, individuals can unlock their potential and pave the path to personal and professional fulfillment.

There are a few elements that must be considered and applied in order to achieve our goals. These are:

Driving Force behind Progress

Taking action serves as the driving force behind progress, acting as the spark that ignites the journey towards our goals. Merely envisioning our desired outcomes is not enough; it is the deliberate and purposeful steps we take that set the wheels of achievement in motion. Without action, goals remain elusive, trapped in the realm of imagination. By understanding that action is the impetus for progress, individuals can break free from the cycle of stagnation and propel themselves towards meaningful accomplishment.

Transforming Intentions into Results

Intentions without action are but empty promises, dormant within the recesses of our minds. It is through action that intentions are transformed into tangible results. Taking that first step, no matter how small, sets in motion a chain reaction that propels us forward. Each subsequent action builds upon the last, accumulating momentum and paving the way to goal attainment. By actively engaging in tasks and initiatives, individuals manifest their desires, turning aspirations into concrete achievements.

Overcoming the Paralysis of Inaction

The specter of inaction looms over many individuals, hindering their progress and thwarting their goals. Fear, doubt, and the allure of comfort often conspire to keep us rooted in inertia. However, by embracing the significance of taking action, we can liberate ourselves from this paralyzing state. Action serves as a counterforce to inaction, breaking the shackles of doubt and propelling us towards our objectives. By stepping outside our comfort zones and embracing the unknown, we open doors to new possibilities, transforming our lives in profound ways.

Learning, Adaptation, and Growth

Action not only propels us towards our goals but also serves as a powerful teacher. Each action we take provides an opportunity for learning, adaptation, and growth. By actively engaging in tasks and initiatives, we acquire valuable insights, refine our strategies, and develop the skills necessary to navigate challenges and overcome obstacles. The process of taking action enables us to learn from our experiences, continuously adapt our approaches, and enhance our abilities, ultimately accelerating our journey towards success.

Building Momentum

The significance of taking action lies in its ability to build momentum. Every action we take generates a ripple effect, generating a powerful current that propels us forward. When small, consistent actions are compounded over time, they generate momentum that is difficult to stop. As momentum builds, it becomes easier to make progress, and achieving objectives becomes a natural consequence. By comprehending this transformative force, individuals can utilize momentum as an ally, propelling them to ever-greater heights of accomplishment.

On the path of our lives, goals are merely figments of our imagination until they are brought to life through action. First steps are always the most challenging. The value of achieving objectives cannot be overstated. By actively engaging in tasks and initiatives, individuals release the force that propels them toward their aspirations, thereby transforming intentions into results, overcoming the paralysis of inaction, fostering learning and growth, and generating unstoppable momentum. As we embrace the power of action, we seize control of our destiny.

LO2: Momentum Accelerators: Discovering Powerful Strategies for Success

Building momentum is a key aspect of achieving success in various areas of life, whether it be in personal endeavors, professional projects, or even larger societal contexts. It provides the energy and drive needed to overcome obstacles and make progress towards our goals. However, building and maintaining momentum can be challenging. We will explore some effective strategies for building momentum and sustaining it over time.

Set Clear and Attainable Goals

One crucial strategy for building momentum is setting clear and attainable goals. Clearly defining what we want to achieve provides a sense of direction and purpose. It helps us focus our efforts and channel our energy towards meaningful outcomes. Setting attainable goals ensures that we experience small victories along the way, which further fuels our motivation and momentum. For example, a SMART goal can be: ***Specific:*** Increase income from $50,000 to $100,000 within the next 12 months. ***Measurable:*** The progress towards the goal can be easily measured by tracking the revenue generated on a monthly or quarterly basis. ***Achievable***: Based on the entrepreneur's current business performance and market opportunities, doubling their income within a year is a challenging yet realistic target. ***Relevant***: Doubling income aligns with the entrepreneur's objective of growing their business and achieving financial success. ***Time-bound:*** The deadline for achieving the goal is set at 12 months, providing a clear timeframe for measuring progress and creating a sense of urgency.

Break Tasks into Manageable Steps

Overwhelming tasks can often hinder our progress and dampen our motivation. To build momentum, it is important to break down large tasks into smaller, manageable steps. By dividing our work into actionable items, we create a sense of progress and accomplishment with each completed step. This incremental approach helps to prevent overwhelm, foster a sense of control, and keep the momentum flowing. For instance, an entrepreneur launching a new business might break down their tasks into segments such as market research, product development, marketing, and sales. By focusing on one step at a time and celebrating milestones along the way, they maintain a sense of progress and momentum. Each completed task provides a boost of confidence and encourages them to tackle the next one.

Harness the Power of Consistency

Consistency is a key ingredient in building momentum. Taking consistent action, even if it is small, ensures that progress is made regularly. By maintaining a steady pace, we avoid stagnation and keep the momentum alive. Whether it's dedicating a specific amount of time each day or completing specific tasks on a regular schedule, consistency helps to build habits and reinforces a positive cycle of progress. Consider a writer aiming to complete a novel. By committing to writing a certain number of words or dedicating a specific amount of time each day, they build momentum in their creative process. The consistent effort gradually moves them closer to their goal. Even on days when inspiration is lacking, their dedication to the routine ensures that progress is made. Over time, this momentum becomes a driving force that propels them towards completing their novel.

Celebrate Milestones and Achievements

Recognizing and celebrating milestones and achievements along the journey is vital to maintaining and amplifying momentum. By acknowledging our progress and rewarding ourselves for the effort invested, we create positive reinforcement that encourages us to continue moving forward. Celebrations can take various forms, such as treating oneself to a small reward, sharing accomplishments with others, or taking a moment to reflect and appreciate how far we have come. These celebrations fuel motivation and serve as reminders of the progress made, strengthening the momentum.

Seek Accountability and Support

Seeking accountability and support from others is a valuable strategy for building momentum. Surrounding yourself with supportive individuals who share your goals and aspirations can greatly enhance your momentum-building efforts. Positive and encouraging relationships provide accountability, motivation, and a sense of community. Engaging with like-minded individuals, whether through networking events, mentorship programs, or online communities, offers support during challenging times and fosters an environment conducive to sustained momentum. An aspiring entrepreneur, for instance, might join a community of fellow entrepreneurs where they share their ideas, set goals, and offer feedback. By engaging with a supportive network, they receive encouragement, constructive criticism, and accountability. This sense of community fosters a positive environment that nurtures momentum and keeps individuals motivated to improve their businesses.

Cultivate a Renewed Mindset

A renewed mind plays a crucial role in building and sustaining momentum.

When we speak of cultivating a renewed mind, we refer to the transformation of our thought patterns and beliefs into ones that are positive, empowering, and growth-oriented. We are able to break free from the shackles of self-doubt, terror, and negativity, which impede our progress, by renewing our minds.

A renewed mind acts as a catalyst for change. It enables us to transcend limitations and embrace opportunities. We develop a sense of clarity, focus, and determination that fuels our actions. It enables us to triumph over difficulties, setbacks, and obstacles with resilience and steadfast perseverance. A clear mind allows us to learn from past mistakes or setbacks, adapt, and maintain progress rather than weighing us down.

Moreover, a refreshed mind fosters a positive outlook and attitude. It allows us to view setbacks as learning and development opportunities. We cultivate the capacity to approach situations with optimism and originality, rather than dwelling on problems. This optimistic perspective inspires and motivates not only us but also those around us. For example, An entrepreneur launching a new product may encounter challenges. By adopting a growth mindset and reframing failures as opportunities for learning and growth, they can maintain a positive outlook. This mindset empowers them to adapt, overcome obstacles, and sustain momentum even in the face of adversity.

Building momentum is a dynamic process that requires a combination of strategies and a renewed mindset. Setting clear goals, breaking tasks into manageable steps, taking consistent action, celebrating achievements, surrounding oneself with a supportive network, and maintaining a positive mindset are all effective strategies for building momentum. By implementing these strategies, individuals can create a powerful force that propels them towards their goals and maximizes their potential for success in their business.

LO3: Effective Success Habits

The decisions we make and the habits we form often determine our success in entrepreneurship, which is a journey of constant growth and innovation. Habits play a crucial role in shaping our daily actions, attitudes, and outcomes. By understanding the power of habit formation and leveraging it to their advantage, entrepreneurs can significantly enhance their chances of success. This section aims to provide entrepreneurs with valuable knowledge and skills related to habit formation, emphasizing how habits can profoundly impact their journey towards success. It explores techniques for developing positive habits that align with goals and support overall progress.

Understanding the Power of Habits

Habits are automatic routines that we engage in without conscious thought. They are deeply ingrained patterns of behavior that shape our lives. While some habits can be detrimental, others can be transformative and empower us to achieve greatness. By acknowledging the influence of habits on our daily lives, entrepreneurs can harness their power and channel it towards positive outcomes.

To effectively create habits that support success, entrepreneurs must first understand the habit loop. The brain creates neural pathways that become stronger with repetition, making the behavior more automatic over time. The habit loop consists of four components: *the cue, the craving, the routine, and the reward.*

Cue: A cue serves as a trigger that initiates the habit. It can be a specific time, location, emotional state, or even an action that precedes the behavior.

Example: Every morning, when the alarm goes off, it serves as a cue to get out of bed and start the day.

Craving: The cue creates a craving or desire for the reward associated with the habit. This craving motivates the individual to engage in the behavior.

Example: Feeling groggy in the morning creates a craving for a cup of coffee to feel awake and alert.

Routine: The routine is the behavior itself—the action or series of actions that form the habit. It can be physical, mental, or emotional.

Example: Drinking a cup of coffee every morning to start the day and feel energized

Reward: The reward is the positive reinforcement that follows the routine. It satisfies the craving and reinforces the habit loop. The reward provides satisfaction or gratification. Rewards can be intrinsic, such as a sense of accomplishment, or extrinsic, such as a treat or recognition.

Example: The caffeine in coffee provides a sense of alertness and satisfaction, which reinforces the habit of drinking coffee in the morning.

By identifying the cues that lead to unproductive or counterproductive routines, entrepreneurs can introduce new cues and routines that align with their goals and aspirations.

Impact of Habits on Success

Habits have a profound impact on an individual's success in various aspects of life. Below are some examples of how habits influence success:

Productivity: Developing habits that promote productivity, such as prioritizing tasks, setting goals, and managing time effectively, can significantly enhance success in professional endeavors. By consistently following a productivity routine, individuals can accomplish more in less time and achieve their goals.

Example: A habit of planning the day's tasks in advance and using time-blocking techniques can help an entrepreneur stay focused, meet deadlines, and make progress on important projects.

Health and Well-Being: Habits related to exercise, nutrition, and self-care contribute to physical and mental well-being. Maintaining healthy habits, such as regular exercise, balanced meals, and sufficient sleep, leads to increased energy, improved cognitive function, and overall better health.

Example: Establishing a habit of exercising for 30 minutes every day, whether through jogging, yoga, or other activities, can enhance physical fitness, reduce stress levels, and boost productivity.

Continuous Learning: Cultivating habits that promote continuous learning and personal development can have a profound impact on success. Regular reading, seeking new knowledge, and embracing a growth mindset contribute to adaptability, innovation, and staying ahead in a rapidly changing world.

Example: Setting aside dedicated time each day for reading or listening to educational podcasts helps entrepreneurs acquire new skills, expand their knowledge base, and gain insights that can be applied to their business strategies.

Networking and Relationship Building: Successful entrepreneurs understand the importance of building strong professional networks and fostering meaningful relationships. Habits that facilitate networking, such as attending industry events, reaching out to contacts, and nurturing connections, can open doors to opportunities and collaborations.

Example: Making it a habit to attend industry conferences or networking events regularly, actively engaging with peers, and following up with contacts afterward can lead to valuable partnerships, mentorship, and business growth.

Positive Mindset and Resilience: Habits related to mindset and resilience greatly impact success. Developing a positive mindset, practicing gratitude, and embracing challenges as opportunities for growth can enhance motivation, creativity, and the ability to overcome obstacles.

Example: Cultivating the habit of journaling and reflecting on daily achievements, positive experiences, and lessons learned can foster a positive mindset, increase self-awareness, and provide the resilience needed.

Activity: Momentum Building Challenge

Objective: To develop practical skills for building momentum towards entrepreneurial success based on the knowledge gained.

Instructions:

Goal Setting and Action Planning:

a. Set a specific and measurable business goal that you would like to achieve within a designated time frame (e.g., increasing sales by 20% in the next three months).

b. Break down the goal into actionable steps or milestones.

c. Create an action plan detailing the tasks, deadlines, and responsible parties for each step.

Momentum-Building Strategies:

a. Identify at least three effective strategies from this chapter that resonate with you for building momentum.

b. Develop a plan to implement these strategies in your business context.

c. Consider how each strategy can be adapted and applied to your specific goal and industry.

Creating Habits for Success:

a. Reflect on your current habits and identify any that may be hindering your progress towards your goal.

b. Select one habit that you want to change or improve to better support your success.

c. Create a habit formation plan, including specific actions, reminders, and accountability measures to establish the desired habit.

Execution and Evaluation:

a. Begin implementing your action plan, executing the tasks and milestones you identified.

b. Track your progress regularly, reviewing and adjusting your plan as necessary.

c. Reflect on the impact of the momentum-building strategies and habit changes on your progress and mindset.

Reflection and Learning:

a. Reflect on the challenges and successes encountered during the activity.

b. Consider how the significance of taking action, effective momentum-building strategies, and supportive habits contributed to your progress.

c. Document key insights and lessons learned from the experience.

Remember, entrepreneurship requires continuous effort and adaptability. By engaging in this practical activity, you will gain hands-on experience applying the concepts of taking action, building momentum, and creating habits that support success. Embrace the journey, stay resilient, and keep the courage to continue pushing forward towards your entrepreneurial goals.

We explored the essential factors that contribute to unlocking a wealth mindset. Throughout the chapter, we emphasized the interconnectedness of these factors and their significance in achieving success. We learned that taking action is crucial for progress and that it builds momentum, propelling us towards our goals. By implementing effective strategies for building momentum, we can sustain our progress and overcome obstacles on our journey to greatness. Additionally, we discovered the importance of cultivating habits that support success. By creating positive habits, we establish routines that align with our goals and increase our chances of achieving them.

It is a continuous journey to unlock a wealth mindset that requires discipline, resilience, and self-awareness. By embracing the power of action, implementing effective strategies for building momentum, and nurturing habits that support success, we can overcome challenges, embrace growth opportunities, and make significant strides towards our goals and aspirations. Remember to apply the knowledge gained to your life and business. Take that first step, leverage the momentum you build, and develop supportive habits. You possess the power to unlock your wealth mindset and embark on a path towards greatness.

In the next chapter, we will explore the significance of scaling a business for long-term success and the cutting-edge strategies to overcome any challenges faced.

CHAPTER 10

Scaling Your Business: Strategies for Sustainable Growth

Scaling a business is not just about expansion; it's about creating a lasting legacy of growth and impact.
—Richard Branson

Learning Objectives

This chapter will help you understand the following factors that are critical to unlocking your wealth mindset:

> **LO1:** Gain knowledge on the concept of scaling a business and its significance for long term success.

> **LO2:** Identify key considerations and challenges when scaling a business.

> **LO3:** Learn effective strategies and best practices for scaling your business successfully.

Achieving sustainable growth is a pivotal goal for entrepreneurs aiming to take their businesses to new heights. As the saying goes, "What got you here won't get you there." The ability to scale a business is a critical milestone in the entrepreneurial journey, as it allows for expansion, increased market presence, and enhanced profitability. However, scaling a business requires careful planning, strategic thinking, and the implementation of effective growth strategies.

Throughout this chapter, you will embark on a journey to understand the essence of scaling a business and its significance for long-term success. By the end, you will have a comprehensive understanding of the key considerations and challenges involved in scaling a business. This will allow you to make informed decisions as you embark on your growth journey.

By absorbing the insights and strategies presented in this chapter, you will be prepared to embark on your scaling journey with confidence. Whether you are expanding into new markets, diversifying your product offerings, or leveraging technology, the knowledge gained will help you navigate the complexities of scaling and lay a solid foundation for sustainable growth.

Get ready to explore the world of scaling your business and unlock the pathways to sustainable growth. Let's dive in and uncover the strategies that will propel your business to new heights!

Unleashing TechNex: Scaling for Lasting Impact and Growth

There was a small software development company named TechNex, started by two passionate entrepreneurs, Lisa and Mark. Their initial goal was to provide custom software solutions to local businesses. As their reputation grew, they realized that they had the potential to scale their business and create a lasting legacy of growth and impact.

Lisa and Mark understood the significance of scaling a business for long-term success. They knew that it went beyond mere expansion. It required careful planning, strategic thinking, and a vision for creating a meaningful impact in their industry and beyond. They embarked on their journey to create a scalable and sustainable business after hearing Richard Branson's words.

To achieve their goal, Lisa and Mark studied successful businesses that have scaled successfully, attended industry conferences, and sought guidance from mentors who had scaled their own companies. They gained knowledge of the various strategies and considerations involved in scaling a business.

Armed with this newfound knowledge, they began implementing the winning strategies and best practices for scaling their business and confronted challenges to ensure a smooth scaling process. They focused on building a strong leadership team, streamlining their operations, and leveraging technology to improve efficiency and productivity.

One of the major challenges they faced was maintaining their company culture as they grew. Lisa and Mark realized that their culture was the foundation of their success, and they couldn't afford to lose it in the process of scaling. They placed great emphasis on fostering an inclusive and collaborative environment where employees feel valued and motivated to contribute their best.

As TechNex scaled, they not only expanded their client base but also diversified their offerings. They recognized emerging trends and identified new opportunities for growth. They invested in research and development, constantly innovating to stay ahead of the competition.

TechNex's commitment to sustainable growth and impact extended beyond their business operations. They actively engaged in corporate social responsibility initiatives, supporting local communities and environmental causes. They believed in creating a positive impact not only within their industry but also in society as a whole.

As the years passed, TechNex became a recognized leader in the software development industry. Their scalable business model, strategic approach, and focus on creating lasting impact set them apart. They had successfully created a legacy of growth and impact.

LO1: The Scaling Revolution: Empowering Businesses for Long-Term Triumphs

Scaling a business is a critical undertaking for entrepreneurs seeking long-term success and sustainable growth. It involves expanding operations, increasing market presence, and maximizing profitability. Understanding the concept of scaling and its significance is paramount to unlocking the full potential of a business. In this section, we will explore the concept of scaling a business and its importance for long-term success.

Concept of Scaling a Business

It is essential to remember that scaling should be a deliberate process, not a random expansion. Businesses must devise growth strategies that align with their vision, mission, and core values. This may require conducting market research, analyzing financial projections, and identifying potential dangers and obstacles.

Scaling a business refers to the strategic and intentional expansion of operations in order to meet rising demand, penetrate new markets, and increase profitability. It goes beyond simple expansion and entails systematically and sustainably increasing the capacity and capabilities of a business. Scaling requires careful planning, the allocation of resources, and the implementation of effective growth strategies.

Significance of Scaling for Long-Term Success

Scaling is crucial for achieving long-term success, as it offers numerous benefits and opportunities for a business. Some of the key reasons why scaling is significant are as follows:

a. Increased Market Presence and Competitive Advantage:

Scaling allows businesses to enter new markets, reach a larger customer base, and establish a stronger presence. By scaling, businesses can gain a competitive advantage over their competitors and position themselves as industry leaders.

b. Enhanced Profitability and Financial Stability:

When a business expands, economies of scale typically occur, which can have a significant impact on profitability and financial stability. Spreading fixed costs over a larger production volume reduces the average cost per unit, resulting in economies of scale. As the company expands and produces more products or services, it is able to negotiate better deals with suppliers, obtain bulk discounts on raw materials or components, and optimize its production processes.

The decrease in average unit costs enables the company to increase its profit margins. With each unit costing less to produce, the company can maintain its selling price while reaping a greater profit per unit. This increased profitability not only generates more revenue but also provides a financial cushion that can be allocated to various initiatives, such as innovation as well as research and development.

c. Attracting Investment and Funding Opportunities:

The process of scaling a business has the potential to attract investment and funding opportunities. One of the most important factors is the inherent growth potential of scalable enterprises. Investors and financiers are frequently attracted to businesses that can demonstrate a clear path to expansion and market share growth. Scaling demonstrates that a company has a firm foundation and the ability to capitalize on market opportunities.

When a company expands, it demonstrates a well-defined and efficient business model. This model illustrates the viability and longevity of the company's operations. It demonstrates how the company generates revenue, acquires and retains customers, and controls expenses. A well-developed business model instills investors and lenders with confidence that their capital will be utilized effectively and generate profitable returns.

Scaling implies an attractive growth trajectory. It demonstrates the company's capacity to capture a larger market share, expand to new locations, or enter new consumer segments. This development potential entices investors and lenders who seek opportunities for substantial investment returns. The prospect of a scalable business experiencing significant expansion may entice those looking to invest money in ventures with high growth potential.

In addition, scaling demonstrates the enterprise's capacity to generate recurring revenue streams. Investors and financiers are attracted to companies with a solid customer base, consistent sales growth, and positive cash flow. Scaling demonstrates that a business has the capacity to manage increased demand and generate revenue at higher volumes, which increases its investment appeal.

Moreover, expanding a business can lead to new funding opportunities. As prospective investment targets, investors such as venture capitalists, private equity firms, and angel investors seek scalable businesses. These investors provide not only capital but also valuable expertise, networks, and direction to aid in the expansion of the business. Scaling a business can also make it a desirable candidate for loans, grants, and government funding programs that target businesses with growth potential.

Case Studies: MercadoLibre

MercadoLibre, often referred to as the "eBay of Latin America," is an Argentinean company that has achieved remarkable success through scaling its operations. Founded in 1999, MercadoLibre initially started as an online marketplace for buying and selling goods in Argentina. However, the company recognized the potential for growth beyond its domestic market and strategically expanded its operations to other countries in South America.

Through a combination of effective growth strategies and a deep understanding of local markets, MercadoLibre successfully scaled its business across the region. The company invested in technological infrastructure, payment solutions, and logistics capabilities to accommodate the unique challenges and needs of each market.

As MercadoLibre scaled, it not only expanded its marketplace services but also diversified its offerings. The company introduced MercadoPago, a digital payment platform that facilitated secure transactions, and MercadoEnvios, a logistics service that streamlined shipping and delivery processes. These additions enhanced the overall user experience and increased customer trust and satisfaction.

By scaling its operations across South America, MercadoLibre established a dominant position in the e-commerce industry, successfully competing with global players like Amazon. Today, MercadoLibre operates in 18 countries and serves millions of users, offering a wide range of products, including electronics, fashion, home goods, and more.

The success of MercadoLibre exemplifies the significance of scaling a business in South America. By expanding its operations beyond borders, adapting to local market dynamics, and continuously innovating, the company was able to achieve long-term success and establish itself as a leading e-commerce platform in the region.

This example demonstrates how scaling a business in South America can open doors to new opportunities, allow for market dominance, and pave the way for sustainable growth and profitability. Entrepreneurs in South America can draw inspiration from MercadoLibre's success story and leverage strategic scaling to unlock the full potential of their businesses in the region and beyond.

Examples of popular international companies that were successful in scaling:

Let's explore a few examples:

a. Amazon

In 1994, Jeff Bezos founded Amazon, a global e-commerce and technology company. The company began as an online bookstore, offering a vast selection and a convenient purchasing experience. In the beginning, Bezos operated Amazon from his garage in Bellevue, Washington.

Amazon began as an online bookstore but grew to become a global e-commerce empire through strategic expansion. Amazon has scaled its business to dominate multiple industries and transform the retail landscape through continuous innovation, expansion into new markets, and diversification of product offerings.

Amazon went public in 1997, and its initial public offering (IPO) signaled the beginning of rapid development and expansion. The company raised capital to invest in infrastructure, technology, and logistics, thereby enhancing its operations and enabling rapid expansion. Amazon continued to diversify its product line and introduced services such as Amazon Prime, which provides subscribers with free shipping and streaming media access.

Amazon expanded internationally throughout the 2000s, launching websites in multiple countries and acquiring businesses to bolster its offerings. Notable acquisitions include the online retailer Zappos in 2009 and the grocery store chain Whole Foods Market in 2017.

Airbnb:

This initial concept evolved into a platform that allows individuals to list their homes, apartments, or spare rooms for short-term rentals, providing travelers with unique and affordable accommodations.

One of the key factors that contributed to Airbnb's rapid scaling was its innovative use of technology. The company developed a user-friendly website and mobile application that made it easy for hosts to list their properties and for travelers to search, book, and review their stays. The platform utilized a review system to establish trust and reliability, allowing hosts and guests to rate and provide feedback on their experiences.

Airbnb disrupted the traditional hospitality industry by scaling its peer-to-peer rental marketplace. By leveraging technology and focusing on user experience, Airbnb rapidly scaled its platform to connect millions of hosts and travelers worldwide, transforming the way people travel and find accommodation.

c. Tesla:

Tesla set out to accelerate the world's transition to sustainable energy. The company's vision was to create electric vehicles that would rival and surpass traditional gasoline-powered cars in terms of performance, range, and desirability.

Tesla, an electric vehicle manufacturer, scaled its operations by investing in research and development, expanding production capabilities, and establishing a network of charging stations. Through visionary leadership and a commitment to sustainable transportation, Tesla scaled its business to become a global leader in the electric vehicle industry.

To support its ambitious goals, Tesla made strategic investments in its manufacturing capabilities. The company established its own production facilities, such as the Tesla Factory in Fremont and several others across the globe. These facilities allowed Tesla to scale up production and meet the increasing demand for its electric vehicles.

Tesla's success in scaling its operations can be attributed to visionary leadership, with Elon Musk leading the charge. Musk's determination, innovative thinking, and ability to inspire a dedicated workforce played a crucial role in Tesla's growth. His focus on long-term goals, such as the development of autonomous driving technology and the integration of renewable energy solutions, has propelled Tesla's position as a global leader in the electric vehicle industry.

LO2: Key Considerations and Challenges Unraveled

Scaling a business is an exciting and transformative process, but it comes with its own set of considerations and challenges. As entrepreneurs aspire to grow their businesses, it is crucial to identify and understand the key factors that can impact successful scaling. In this essay, we will explore the important considerations and challenges that entrepreneurs need to be aware of when scaling a business.

Considerations When Scaling a Business

Scaling a business requires thoughtful planning and consideration of various factors. Here are some key considerations that entrepreneurs should keep in mind:

a. Market Demand and Potential

To understand current market demand, it is important to consider future trends and potential opportunities. Technological advancements, changes in consumer behavior, and regulatory developments all constantly influence market dynamics. Assessing the potential for growth involves identifying emerging trends, evaluating their impact on the industry, and positioning the business to capitalize on these opportunities. This forward-looking approach enables businesses to stay ahead of the curve and anticipate future demand.

Identifying the target audience is crucial for scaling successfully. This involves profiling potential customers and understanding their needs, preferences, and purchasing behavior. By gaining insights into the target audience, businesses can tailor their marketing strategies, product development, and customer experience to meet specific demands. This targeted approach enhances the chances of capturing a larger market share and sustaining growth.

Another aspect of assessing market potential is evaluating the competitive landscape. Analyzing competitors helps identify their strengths, weaknesses, and unique selling propositions. Understanding the competitive environment allows businesses to position themselves effectively, differentiate their offerings, and develop strategies to gain a competitive advantage. It also helps identify any gaps in the market that can be exploited through innovative products, superior customer service, or disruptive business models.

b. Scalable Business Model

It is essential to evaluate the scalability of your business model. A scalable business model not only enables the management of increased demand and expansion but also provides a competitive advantage in a market that is dynamic and constantly changing. Businesses that can efficiently scale are better positioned to seize new opportunities and adapt to shifting market conditions. Scalability fosters resilience, allowing businesses to withstand economic downturns or sudden shifts in consumer preferences. Moreover, a scalable business model frequently attracts potential investors and stakeholders because it demonstrates the potential for substantial investment returns and long-term growth prospects. By systematically evaluating and refining the scalability of your business model, you pave the way for long-term success and the realization of your organization's vision for the future.

c. Financial Resources

Scaling a business often requires significant financial investments. Evaluate the financial resources available and determine if additional funding or capital is necessary to support the scaling process. Consider the financial implications of hiring new employees, expanding infrastructure, marketing efforts, and inventory management.

d. Operational Efficiency and Processes

When preparing to expand your business, it is essential to conduct a comprehensive analysis of operational efficacy and processes. Scaling has the potential to magnify your organization's current inefficiencies, making it imperative to streamline and optimize operations prior to expansion. Conduct a thorough analysis of your workflows, systems, and technology infrastructure in order to identify potential obstacles to scaling. Introduce process enhancements, automation, and lean methods to increase productivity and decrease waste. Moreover, consider investing in scalable and adaptable technological solutions that can accommodate increased volume and complexity. By enhancing operational efficiency, you not only assure smooth expansion, but also lay the foundation for long-term success and enhanced performance.

Challenges When Scaling a Business

Scaling a business is an ambitious and exhilarating endeavor that represents the fulfillment of an entrepreneur's vision for development and success. As a business expands its operations, enters new markets, and gains a larger customer base, it enters an exhilarating phase of development. However, the path of transformation is not without obstacles. Challenges proliferate when scaling a business, requiring entrepreneurs and their teams to demonstrate strategic planning, adaptability, and tenacity. Below are some common challenges that arise when expanding a business and emphasize the most important considerations and solutions for overcoming these obstacles. By recognizing and navigating these obstacles, entrepreneurs can pave the way for sustainable growth and capitalize on the vast opportunities that accompany successful scaling.

a. Human Resources and Talent Acquisition

The importance of human resources and talent procurement cannot be overstated as a business grows in size. Building a skilled and devoted workforce capable of propelling the company's expansion is essential for the scaling process to be successful. Attracting top talent becomes a priority because the right individuals possess the knowledge and creativity required to successfully navigate the challenges of expansion. Attracting qualified candidates requires an effective talent procurement strategy that includes a compelling employer brand, well-written job descriptions, and an efficient recruitment process. To equip employees with the skills and knowledge they need to excel in their duties and contribute to the company's success, it is crucial to provide comprehensive training and development opportunities upon hiring.

In addition, establishing solid management structures is essential for effectively leading and coordinating a growing workforce. A positive and supportive work environment encourages employee engagement and retention, thereby reducing turnover rates and associated hiring expenses. Moreover, instituting performance management systems and clear career progression pathways can motivate employees and demonstrate an organization's commitment to their growth and development.

b. Maintaining Quality and Consistency

When expanding a business, maintaining quality and consistency is of the utmost importance, as they directly affect consumer satisfaction and brand reputation. As operations expand, there may be an increase in demand for products or services, putting pressure on production and service delivery. If not managed diligently, this increased burden could result in quality lapses. To address this difficulty, it is essential to implement stringent quality control measures. Regular inspections, testing, and adherence to industry standards enable the identification and correction of any deviations from the intended quality standards.

Standardized processes play a crucial role in maintaining uniformity throughout all business operations. Documenting and streamlining workflows ensures that each stage is carried out consistently, regardless of the volume of work. This reduces errors and variations in the final product, enhancing the dependability of the company's products. Moreover, scalable technology solutions can aid in automating processes, reducing the likelihood of human errors, and enhancing overall productivity.

Maintaining quality and consistency is also dependent on effective communication and collaboration between teams. Different departments and teams may operate independently as the business expands, leading to miscommunication and misunderstandings. Establishing explicit communication channels, fostering interdepartmental collaboration, and promoting a culture of open feedback promote organizational alignment and cohesion.

c. Scalable Infrastructure and Technology

To successfully navigate the complexities of scaling a business, a firm foundation of scalable infrastructure and technology is essential. As the customer base grows and the scope and complexity of operations increase, obsolete or inadequate technology can become a significant bottleneck. In the absence of a forward-thinking technology infrastructure, sluggish response times, system failures, and data saturation are just a few of the issues that may arise.

Investing in scalable technology solutions provides the business with the adaptability required to meet growing demands. Cloud-based services, for example, offer the benefit of on-demand resources, enabling businesses to scale up or down as required without incurring significant capital expenditures. In addition, cloud-based platforms facilitate seamless collaboration between teams and enhance access to vital data from multiple locations.

d. Market Competition and Differentiation

In a rapidly expanding market, competition can become intense, making differentiation a crucial success factor for a business that is scaling. Understanding the target audience and their changing needs is essential for effectively tailoring offerings to suit their specific needs. Thorough market research identifies market gaps and reveals unmet consumer demands, thereby revealing opportunities for innovation and differentiation.

To differentiate themselves from rivals, businesses must effectively communicate their unique value proposition. Not only does articulating what differentiates their products, services, or brand from others attract potential customers, but it also encourages brand loyalty among existing consumers. This differentiation may be based on a variety of factors, including superior product quality, exceptional customer service, innovative features, or a compelling brand narrative that resonates with consumers.

In Summary, the expansion of a business is an exciting journey with both opportunities and obstacles. Entrepreneurs can make informed decisions and navigate the path to successful growth by identifying and comprehending the key factors and obstacles involved in scaling. Consideration of market demand, scalability, financial resources, and operational efficacy assists in establishing a solid foundation for scaling. Additionally, it is essential for long-term success to be prepared to face challenges relating to talent acquisition, quality maintenance, technology infrastructure, and competition. Entrepreneurs can confidently embark on the scaling journey, positioning their businesses for long-term growth and prosperity, if they have a thorough understanding of these factors and obstacles.

LO3: Accelerate Your Business: Learn the Keys to Sustainable Growth

Scaling a business is an exciting yet challenging endeavor. It requires careful planning, strategic decision-making, and the implementation of effective strategies and best practices. We will explore the key strategies and practices that can help businesses navigate the path to successful scaling.

Develop a Clear Vision and strategy

One of the fundamental steps in scaling a business is having a clear vision and strategy. Define your long-term goals and identify the direction you want your business to take. A well-defined strategy will serve as a roadmap for growth and guide your decisions along the way.

Build a Strong Organizational Structure

It is crucial to establish a solid organizational structure as your business grows. A solid organizational structure provides the framework for efficient decision-making, streamlined operations, and sustained growth. Employees are better able to comprehend their specific contributions and areas of accountability when roles and responsibilities are clearly defined. This clarity promotes a sense of ownership and independence, thereby enhancing individual and team performance.

Streamlining communication channels is crucial to ensuring that information circulates efficiently between departments and levels. Open and transparent communication improves collaboration, reduces misunderstandings, and enables the rapid resolution of any scaling-related challenges.

In addition, aligning the team with the company's vision and values fosters a sense of shared purpose. Mission-aligned employees are more likely to be motivated, engaged, and committed to attaining shared goals.

Invest in Your Team

Investing in your staff is crucial to the future success of your growing business. As the organization's backbone, a competent and inspired team can make all the difference in attaining ambitious growth objectives. Attracting top personnel requires competitive compensation packages as well as a dynamic work environment that places a premium on employee development and well-being. In a rapidly evolving business environment, it is essential to provide ongoing training and professional development opportunities to keep your team's skills and knowledge current.

A culture that encourages open communication, collaboration, and innovation is essential for cultivating a highly engaged and devoted workforce. Encourage a workplace where employees' ideas are valued and they feel empowered to share their perspectives. Recognize and reward team members' accomplishments to foster a sense of appreciation and motivation. Moreover, promoting work-life balance and wellness initiatives demonstrates that you care about your employees' well-being, resulting in increased job satisfaction and loyalty.

Your team will be the propelling force behind the expansion of your business. By investing in the growth of your team and fostering a positive work environment, you can cultivate a high-performing and devoted workforce that will propel your business to new heights. The collective effort and dedication of a well-supported team will not only enable your business to meet the challenges of scaling but also position it for long-term growth and prosperity.

Embrace Technology and Automation

Embracing technology and automation is not only advantageous but necessary for success in the fast-paced and competitive environment of expanding enterprises. Automation streamlines repetitive tasks, freeing up employees' time to concentrate on more strategic, growth-driving activities. Whether it's automating order processing, inventory management, or customer support, technology enables businesses to efficiently manage increased obligations.

Investing in a dependable customer relationship management (CRM) system enables organizations to manage and analyze customer interactions, thereby facilitating personalized and targeted marketing strategies. In turn, this improves the customer experience and fosters customer loyalty, which is essential for recurrent business and positive word-of-mouth referrals.

Cloud-based solutions offer the necessary flexibility and scalability during periods of accelerated expansion. They enable businesses to access data and software from any location, thereby facilitating collaboration among geographically dispersed teams. In addition, cloud computing reduces infrastructure costs and eliminates the need for large initial hardware investments.

Tools for data analytics play a crucial role in acquiring valuable insights from immense quantities of data. Customer behavior, market trends, and operational performance analysis can reveal growth opportunities and inform strategic decision-making. Utilizing data-driven insights enables businesses to maintain a competitive advantage, anticipate customer requirements, and continuously enhance their offerings.

Focus on Customer Experience

The key to long-term success is a relentless focus on the consumer experience. As the consumer base grows, their preferences and requirements may change, making it essential to remain sensitive to their comments and anticipations. Implementing periodic surveys, conducting market research, and closely monitoring customer interactions can provide invaluable insight into enhancement and innovation opportunities. Businesses can ensure that their offerings remain pertinent and compelling in a competitive market by modifying their products or services in response to customer feedback.

Developing robust customer relationships is also crucial. Invest in personalized interactions and responsive support to foster trust and brand loyalty. Customers who are satisfied not only become repeat purchasers but also fervent brand advocates. Customers often share their positive experiences with their friends, family, and online communities, thereby contributing to organic growth and expanding the customer base.

Additionally, it is essential to emphasize excellent customer service. Responding quickly to inquiries and efficiently resolving issues demonstrates a dedication to customer satisfaction. Going the extra mile to exceed expectations can cultivate brand loyalty and leave a lasting impression.

Establish Strategic Partnerships

Establishing strategic partnerships can be a game-changer for effectively and efficiently expanding your business. By forming partnerships with complementary businesses or industry leaders, you gain access to numerous resources, information, and market opportunities that would be difficult to acquire on your own. Strategic partners can provide invaluable insight into new markets, allowing you to gain a deeper understanding of local preferences and consumer behavior. In addition, these partnerships can open the door to dormant distribution channels, allowing your products or services to reach a larger audience more quickly.

The advantages of strategic alliances extend beyond short-term gains; they can promote long-term growth and sustainability. By leveraging one another's strengths, businesses can more effectively navigate challenges and capitalize on emergent opportunities. In the ever-changing landscape of scaling, a well-curated network of partners can function as a force multiplier, propelling your business to new heights.

Monitor Key Metrics and Adapt

Monitoring key performance indicators is essential for guiding a successful scaling strategy. Tracking relevant KPIs such as revenue growth, profit margins, customer acquisition costs, customer retention rates, and inventory turnover provides a clear picture of your company's performance as it grows. Analysis of these metrics on a regular basis enables the identification of trends and patterns, highlighting areas of strength and those that require refinement.

A company that is expanding must make decisions based on data. Utilize the insights obtained from monitoring KPIs to make strategic, well-informed decisions. Consider reallocating resources to more efficient channels if certain marketing channels produce high customer acquisition costs. If conversion rates are lower than anticipated, you should evaluate the user experience and implement changes to increase conversion rates. Being proactive in data analysis and strategy adaptation positions your business to quickly capture opportunities and address challenges.

During the process of scaling, agility and adaptability are crucial qualities. Being responsive to changing market conditions and evolving consumer preferences can be the difference between thriving and stagnating. Adopt a culture of continuous learning and development in which teams are encouraged to experiment, test, and iterate. Adaptability enables a business to stay ahead of the curve and relevant in a competitive environment.

In conclusion, scaling a business successfully requires a combination of effective strategies and best practices. By developing a clear vision, building a strong organizational structure, investing in your team, embracing technology, prioritizing customer experience, establishing strategic partnerships, and monitoring key metrics, you can pave the way for sustainable growth. Remember, scaling is an iterative process that requires continuous learning and adjustment. By adopting these strategies and practices, you can position your business for long-term success in an ever-evolving business landscape.

The Role of Innovation, Continuous Improvement and Adaptation to Scaling

Innovation, continuous improvement, and adaptability are essential elements in scaling a business successfully. These elements cannot be overemphasized. They play vital roles in navigating the challenges and seizing opportunities that arise during the growth process. Let's take a closer look at each of these factors and their significance:

Innovation

Innovation drives growth and differentiation. It is essential for addressing urgent global challenges and societal requirements. In order to create a more sustainable and equitable world in the face of complex problems such as climate change, resource scarcity, and healthcare issues, innovative solutions are essential. By promoting research and development in fields such as renewable energy, healthcare technology, and education, innovation has the potential to revolutionize entire industries and enhance the quality of life for people worldwide.

In addition, innovation fosters collaboration and knowledge-sharing among individuals, organizations, and nations, thereby creating a network of forward-thinking individuals who endeavor to improve the world. Innovation promotes not only economic development but also a brighter and more promising future for humanity.

Continuous Improvement

Continuous improvement is the ongoing effort to incrementally improve processes, products, or services.

In addition to efficiency advances, continuous improvement fosters a culture of learning within an organization. Inviting employees to actively participate in the development process encourages a sense of ownership and engagement. Individuals are more invested in the success of a business when they feel empowered to contribute their ideas and insights. This collaborative approach not only generates innovative solutions, but also fosters a dynamic and positive workplace where employees feel valued and motivated.

In addition, continuous improvement is an effective risk management instrument. Businesses can proactively identify potential bottlenecks, vulnerabilities, and compliance issues by assessing and refining their processes on a regular basis. By addressing these issues early on, organizations can mitigate risks and avoid costly future errors or setbacks.

Furthermore, continuous development extends beyond internal operations to supplier and partner relationships. By collaborating closely with stakeholders, businesses can improve communication, expedite supply chains, and construct more robust and dependable networks. This collaborative strategy supports trust and loyalty, resulting in lasting partnerships and a mutually beneficial ecosystem.

Adaptability

Adaptability is the ability to adjust and respond effectively to changing circumstances. Embracing adaptability as a core value fosters a culture of innovation and experimentation within an organization. It encourages employees to think creatively, take calculated risks, and strive for continuous improvement. When members of a team are receptive to change and view obstacles as growth opportunities, they become more resilient and better equipped to face future uncertainties.

Adaptability is also closely related to customer-centricity. Businesses that prioritize adaptability are more attuned to the shifting requirements and preferences of their customers. Adaptable companies can tailor their products and services to remain relevant and maintain a competitive advantage by actively listening to customer feedback, analyzing market trends, and monitoring industry developments. This customer-centric strategy strengthens client relationships, fosters brand loyalty, and opens the door to new market segments.

Furthermore, adaptability is crucial to talent management and employee fulfillment. Offering opportunities for professional development and advancement is essential to attracting and retaining top talent in a dynamic business environment. Companies that prioritize adaptability foster a stimulating and demanding work environment in which employees are encouraged to evolve and contribute to the success of the organization. Consequently, businesses that are adaptable are in a better position to attract high-caliber individuals who are eager to develop with the company.

The interplay of innovation, continuous improvement, and adaptability is crucial for scaling a business successfully. Innovation drives the development of new ideas and solutions, enabling businesses to differentiate themselves and create value. Continuous improvement ensures that processes and operations are optimized, leading to efficiency and effectiveness in delivering products or services. Adaptability allows businesses to respond to market changes, customer demands, and competitive challenges, ensuring they remain agile and resilient in the face of growth.

Together, these factors foster a culture of growth, agility, and responsiveness. By embracing innovation, continuously improving operations, and remaining adaptable, businesses can not only scale successfully but also position themselves as industry leaders. As they grow, businesses should prioritize these elements to drive sustainable expansion, maintain a competitive edge, and create long-term value for their stakeholders.

Activity:
Assessing the Scalability of Your Business

Objective:

The objective of this activity is to help entrepreneurs evaluate the scalability of their business. By going through a series of questions and considerations, this activity will enable entrepreneurs to assess the potential for growth and scalability within their current business model.

Instructions:

Review the Business Model:

Take a close look at your existing business model and assess its scalability potential. Consider factors such as the target market, product or service offerings, revenue streams, and cost structure.

Ask yourself: Is my business model flexible and adaptable to accommodate growth? Are there any inherent limitations or constraints that may hinder scalability?

Analyze Market Demand:

Evaluate the market demand for your product or service. Research industry trends, customer preferences, and the overall growth potential of your target market.

Ask yourself: Is there a significant and sustainable market demand for my offering? Are there opportunities to expand into new customer segments or geographic locations?

Assess Operational Capacity:

Evaluate your current operational capacity and infrastructure. Consider factors such as production capabilities, supply chain management, distribution channels, and the scalability of resources.

Ask yourself: Can my operations handle increased demand without compromising quality or efficiency? Are there potential bottlenecks or limitations that may hinder scaling?

Evaluate Financial Resources:

Assess the financial resources available to support scaling efforts. Consider factors such as access to capital, financial stability, and potential sources of funding for expansion.

Ask yourself: Do I have the necessary financial resources to support scaling activities? Are there alternative funding options available to fuel growth?

Consider Scalable Business Practices:

Review your existing business practices and identify areas that can be optimized for scalability. Evaluate aspects such as automation, technology integration, scalability of processes, and scalability of the workforce.

Ask yourself: Are there opportunities to automate or streamline processes to accommodate increased volume? Can technology be leveraged to scale more efficiently? Do I have the ability to scale the workforce when needed?

Reflect on Competitive Advantage:

Analyze your competitive advantage and differentiation factors in the market. Consider factors such as unique value propositions, barriers to entry, and potential for sustainable competitive advantage.

Ask yourself: Do I have a competitive advantage that can be leveraged during scaling? Are there any barriers to entry that protect my business from competitors?

Determine Growth Potential:

Based on your assessments and reflections, determine the growth potential of your business. Consider the scalability of your business model, market demand, operational capacity, financial resources, scalable business practices, and competitive advantage.

Ask yourself: On a scale of 1 to 5 (1 being low and 5 being high), how would you rate the scalability potential of your business? What factors contribute to this rating?

Conclusion:

By engaging in this activity, entrepreneurs can gain a clearer understanding of the scalability potential of their businesses. It provides a structured framework to assess key factors and prompts critical thinking about the feasibility and potential roadblocks to scaling. Based on the outcomes of this activity, entrepreneurs can then make informed decisions, identify areas for improvement, and develop strategies to enhance scalability and fuel sustainable growth.

In this chapter, we explored the concept of scaling a business and its significance for long-term success. It was highlighted that Scaling a business involves expanding its operations and achieving sustainable growth. We discussed how scaling is different from mere growth in that it requires careful planning and strategic decision-making to ensure long-term success.

Scaling allows businesses to unlock their full potential, tap into new markets, increase profitability, and create a sustainable competitive advantage.

In addition, expanding a business necessitates a comprehensive understanding of its fundamental capabilities and resources. Identifying and capitalizing on these assets is essential for a successful expansion.

We examined the key considerations and challenges that businesses face when scaling. Factors such as market demand, operational capacity, financial resources, talent acquisition, and infrastructure were discussed. It is crucial for businesses to assess these considerations and proactively address challenges to ensure a smooth scaling process.

The expansion of a business necessitates a comprehensive evaluation of market dynamics and customer requirements. By maintaining market awareness, businesses can proactively identify trends, capitalize on emerging opportunities, and effectively position themselves against competitors.

To scale a business successfully, we explored effective strategies and best practices. These included developing a clear vision and strategy, building a strong organizational structure, investing in the team, embracing technology and automation, focusing on customer experience, establishing strategic partnerships, and monitoring key metrics. These strategies provide a solid foundation for businesses to navigate the complexities of scaling and achieve sustainable growth.

By understanding the concept of scaling, recognizing the key considerations and challenges, and implementing effective strategies and best practices, businesses can position themselves for long-term success. Scaling requires a wealth mindset where entrepreneurs and business leaders are open to innovation, continuous improvement, and adaptability. It is an iterative process that demands resilience, agility, and a commitment to learning and evolving.

As you continue your journey toward scaling your business, remember to revisit the concepts and strategies discussed in this chapter. Apply them in your own context, adapt them to your specific industry or market, and continue to seek new knowledge and insights. Scaling a business is a dynamic and ongoing process, and by leveraging the knowledge and skills gained, you can overcome challenges, seize opportunities, and create a thriving and sustainable business. Best wishes!!

About the Author

Tannizia Gasper is a financial luminary on a mission to transform how people perceive and interact with money. Her journey in the dynamic world of banking has been marked by her unwavering belief in the philosophy, "I can be anything I put my mind to" In addition to being a seasoned professional, she is also a devoted wife and mother of two young girls, roles she values with equal fervour. Mrs. Gasper's career in the financial industry has honed her expertise in finance and business, allowing her to guide countless individuals toward realizing their entrepreneurial aspirations and expanding their enterprises. Her transformative effect on her clients is fuelled by her unrelenting pursuit of knowledge in business, human behavior, and finance. Tannizia Gasper is well-equipped to provide her clients with innovative solutions and tangible results due to her insatiable thirst for knowledge and dedication to remaining at the vanguard of her field. Her devotion to her clients is a vocation, not merely a commitment. Tannizia strives ceaselessly to exceed expectations, ensuring that each client receives not only exceptional service but also an atmosphere in which they feel sincerely welcomed and valued. Her advocacy for females in her community extends beyond her professional endeavours. She works tirelessly as the coordinator of an active girl's organization to provide a supportive and empowering environment for young women to flourish and realize their full potential. Her dedication to cultivating the next generation of leaders exemplifies her zeal for positive change. Tannizia Gasper's life is a transformative force of a growth mindset, and her mission to change people's perspectives on money is more than a job; it's a calling. Tannizia is not only changing lives through her commitment to lifelong learning, unwavering dedication to her clients, and advocacy for the empowerment of young females; she is also shaping a brighter future for all. Her story inspires those who strive to make their dreams a reality and leave a lasting mark on their community and the world.

www.ingramcontent.com/pod-product-compliance
Lightning Source LLC
Chambersburg PA
CBHW071211210326
41597CB00016B/1764